I KNOW WHY
Young Men
RAGE

I KNOW WHY
Young Men
RAGE

THOMAS JOHNSON

The Benevolent Tinker

Copyright © 2020 by Thomas Johnson.

Library of Congress Control Number:	2020913950

HARDBACK:	978-1-952155-73-4
PAPERBACK:	978-1-952155-72-7
EBOOK:	978-1-952155-74-1

All rights reserved. No part of this publication may be reproduced, distributed, or transmitted in any form or by any electronic or mechanical means, without the prior written permission of the publisher, except in the case of brief quotations embodied in critical reviews and certain other noncommercial uses permitted by copyright law.

Ordering Information:

For orders and inquiries, please contact:
1-888-404-1388
www.goldtouchpress.com
book.orders@goldtouchpress.com

Printed in the United States of America

Contents

Introduction ix

Chapter 1: Living By What We Know 1
Chapter 2: How Did We Let Things Get So Bad? 13
Chapter 3: Feminine Surrender 25
Chapter 4: I Know Why Young Men Rage 41
Chapter 5: It's All In The Voice You Hear 53
Chapter 6: We Are All Broken 63
Chapter 7: The Voice We Know 71
Chapter 8: The Life You Keep 79
Chapter 9: Learning The Welcome 89
Chapter 10: Finding The Inner Child 99
Chapter 11: Keeping Watch 109
Chapter 12: Are We There Yet? 117

Epilogue 129

A Dedication To Live For:

A miracle demands nothing of us.
It only invites us to come and see and be part of the wonder.
The Benovolent Tinker

Introduction

In today's world we've experienced a tragic loss of good meaningful values because society has lost its focus on where relationships begin and end. Reaching out to be loved and to love someone else has become a fearful event in everyday life.

Women need to be loved by men; men are to love women, who were created for men to walk with them and be cherished by them. With all the apprehension between men and women the beautiful love they are meant to share is in question. God created love and deemed it good; man and woman have made it into something quite opposite. Without the loving example of the man and woman children have become isolated. This is something we have grown accustom too because that is what we remember.

The meaning of the family unit is being questioned. The roles of father and mother do not have a place of importance in the raising of children in America; the land of the free and the home of the brave. In doubt and fear men run from the brokenness of their families and hide in their sorrows. Women are so used to it that marriage is barely considered important anymore. When husbands and fathers leave physically or emotionally masculine empowerment leaves with them.

The result of husbandless wives and fatherless children is the people we have become: wives have lost hope, sons don't know how to show love to the women or how to be loved by another man and daughters don't know how to surrender to a man's love and give it back again, women don't know how to commune as a society with other women. The grace of feminine community is a quandary.

The family structure is so fractured that we have little understanding of what it means to have a fulfilling and meaningful relation with those of the same or opposite sex. A father cannot be a mother, nor can a mother be a father, grandparents were not meant to raise their grandchildren. Yes, wives will carry on when their husbands leave them physically, and husbands will muddle through when their wives decide that mothering wasn't what they thought it would be. The result is too many broken people unsure of everything and living in fear, torn inside and tearing each other up. We have lost the ability to reach out to others when they are hurting and we get lost in our own feeling of isolation.

This terror hinders us from receiving God's love and loving others. We need to turn to the source of life and hope, Jesus our Savior and reach out to each other again in holy caring love.

The story teller's lips have been silent to long in America. It is the hour of change and time to live the story of God's love again.

It is long past time we start our way back to our heavenly Father as a people and as a nation; as a world. We ought not delay a moment longer. As a society we are desperately lost in our technology. We need to come to grips that we talk how we listen. We are not listening at all. We are not talking at all. The lost art of conversation is evidence of this very fact. Texting is not talking. Skyeping and chat room chatting is not talking or seeing the other person as a person. A conversation without the effect of human contact is not a conversation. It is something far less that only brings us to harm. Technology is a tool of communication but we cannot let the tool speak for us to each other in the matters of human connection. A little black box with even smaller black buttons cannot constitute as family. It won't hug you back and doesn't see your tears when you cry, or feel your hurt when you are in pain.

A person in your day becomes a blur or a sound blurp on the horizon of your day when you only see a devise that you let do the talking for you. When we talk our words need to mean something for us to be complete. And that can only be accomplished by a personal interaction with another human being.

God created in us with the need for conversation with Him and with each other. When that is broken we are indeed lost and isolated and overcome by fear of aloneness.

The price we are paying is the loss of community and family and ability to feel anything real as we get lost in the virtual reality. So remember the computer is a machine.

Your cell phone is machine. Your video game is a machine without a soul or without a care for how you feel. A personal relationship with Jesus our Savior and with other people is the only stuff that will keep you healthy, happy and whole. As for technology make it work for you, not for you. Listen to the wind. To your heart beating. The birds that sing. The people who sing their heart song to you. Listen to life and live.

The lullabies we heard way back when or the ones we wish we could have heard are waiting to be heard and heard again and will stand by until our last breath; as will the quiet uneventful walks taken and the spontaneous silly conversations we may have had. They are the missing puzzle pieces of who we are. What has become "normal" family communication will never replace them. A cell phone won't hug you back.

We need face to face voice consolation in our times of despair. We need the face to face voice of comfort that shoos away the monsters under the bed and in the closet. This comfort is what God intended for us but it is getting lost in our day; in our moments. When these comforts are missing in a child's life he or she struggles to grow.

The human soul is tuned to all that is right and wrong for we know that there is a right and wrong but we need a compass of direction to hold on too to find the good in life and it can only be found in the only one who can save and keep us, Jesus the Christ; for the individual, the family, the community, our nation, and the world.

We learn how to ask and receive by what we see and hear. With our present mind set of faster and more and more the important life lessons have been halted and are less and less. Yet and still, God finds a way to us in our questions of loss and isolation to speak to our need to give an answer to what plagues us. The answers begin with knowing where we began and where we left off in the conversation with God and man and woman and child. The trail to find them again are in the missing people and moments that are still waiting to rejoin us once again. God's light of heaven on earth, Jesus the Christ. Our renewed relationship back to our Father in heaven is through Him exclusively and completely, the Son of man/ Son of God-God with us, Emanuel.

We all need to know that there is something better for 'us. We need someone to hope in. We all need to hear words of life, and love. These words are in the gift of enlightened hearing of the voice of the Great Shepherd Jesus the Messiah come and He will speak to you right where you are. I know that there is so much loneliness and fear that overwhelms us day to day, but we have a friend who is bigger, smarter, and stronger. I have been there. These are the moments of my way back through the valley of the shadow of death. I offer them to you. Thank you for being a part of my journey.

CHAPTER 1

Living By What We Know

People go with what they are taught by others; this is common knowledge. But we learn the most important things by what we don't see and can't hear, by the questions that follow. The void of our presumed existence helps lead our seeking souls and inquiring minds to their destination: the answer; A Savior who loved us first and wants us back just as we are.

We may hear many voices, but there is only one voice that can save us: the gentle voice of the Great Shepherd, Jesus the Christ. And as we turn to His presence through that tiny little crack of light in our soul the crack becomes wider and wider the closer we draw to Him; as the door to our hearts opens moment by moment, one small miracle at a time. His hand reaches into our welcome and then He draws us into His wonder of heaven on earth; His presence of peace and rest. In the warmth of the presence of Jesus the sleepy child awakens and steps into the light of new day. His Holy Spirit comes into our heart to make it His home and the darkness that was, melts away and the child that was dead in the sleep of sin breathes life, His life, and lives again.

From the beginning of our lives, God planted a seed of truth that will never go away; the truth is that He is God and we are not.

Psalm 39:4-6 tells us

Lord make me to know my end, And what is the measure of my days, That I may know how frail I am. Indeed you have made my days as handbreadths, And my age is nothing before you. Selah-Surely every man walks about like a shadow; Surely they busy themselves in vain; He heaps up riches, And does not know who will gather them. (Psalm 119: 105 NKJV)

The battle between good and evil, light and darkness is a constant struggle that will continue until the last soul to be reborn is returned to the loving arms of The Great Shepherd, Jesus the Christ. The truth is that this is His fight and only He can daily win it for us and through us. He is the ever present Living Word of God. Jesus overcame this world of sin, sickness, death, and the grave. He is our champion. We can try to do things our own way, but the battle over sin and death is too great a fight for us, we will fail and fall on our own. However, if and when we do fall He is there to pick us up again and again and carry us to the other side.

We cause pain for ourselves and others in our life when we resist the Savior's loving care.

When we fall others may fall with us, as our hurt is put upon them, for they are all on the path with us. But the forgiveness from the God Who Forgives is there waiting to lift every broken heart to heal and restore that which was lost and give back life to those once dead that they may dwell in His peace and rest now and forever. Amen.

The erring of one man and one woman brought sin, destruction, and death upon all the generations forth coming. Paradise was lost in Eden yet and still God's plan of redemption, the Second Adam come had already begun to bring all persons born back to Him. I know it is difficult for finite beings to understand His plan in His timing, yet we can ask as beloved children to know His plan. He will lead us into the mystery of His love for us, one moment at a time.

It was because of the fall of Adam (the man and the woman), that our fellowship with God needed to be restored. The reunion of one soul come back home to the heavenly Father is jubilation of celebration in heaven by all of God's angels. And even greater the joy when a family comes to know the saving grace of Jesus the Christ. The faithfulness of one man and one woman standing together in the faith of the Lord Jesus, by the power of His Holy Spirit is an awesome stronghold on earth. Indeed the healing of a son and daughter is paramount to the healing of all generations both now and into the future.

There is only one solution to this break with God; put the Son of God back into the man and the woman and the children and creation will follow. The man will have the power and the strength to stand against the darkness without and within and the woman will have the strength and power to stand with him. Having done all to stand, stay standing.

When a man takes stand in his life, he needs to know how to stand, and as strange as it sounds, the best way for him to stand is to kneel all the better with the woman at his side before the Lord with one heart.

Our hurried age has taken us too far too fast. The family needs an anchor. A man and woman of faith in Jesus fit the bill nicely. Our best allies are the people who knows us best. God put them in our lives to help us when we are down or fallen and hurting.

There is one rule in the battle against the principalities of darkness: never think you can fight the battle of faith on your own. Here's a question for you: "What is the first thing you see before going into battle?" If you answered the enemy, by your own words you have already lost the fight.

The first thing you should see is the army that stands at your side, the men and women who have your back. The first great victory of your life is to understand that you don't have the answers to life's questions, nor does anyone else. But if you turn to others and admit your lack of understanding and turn together to the smartest of all, God, you will know what you need to know when you need to know it together as one heart and one mind (Matthew 18:20).

We need to act in the stead of those we are called to love. But first we need a plan to accomplish the task before us. Remember this is God's plan. If the man and woman stand hand in hand, in faith believing that the Lord Jesus is able to do all things, they can accomplish all things by the power of His love and walking in the leading of His Holy Spirit. All things are possible with God. God is a present help in the time of need (Psalm 46: 1).

A wonderful miracle happens when we turn to each other and together turn to Jesus our Savior: the void we felt inside becomes filled with His love, joy, and peace. Our darkened souls are flooded with heaven's light, and we can see again. We see those we thought we knew and are changed. The painful things we allowed into our, heart, mind, and soul become less painful as we walk in Jesus. His strength to love in us becomes greater. God's everlasting forgiveness and love will cast out fear of seeing who we were. We will grow in His mercy and grace; there is no condemnation to those who are in Christ Jesus (Romans 8:1).

In our brokenness we will able to see those whom we have missed: our spouses, our children, the people that care about us. The faces that were turned away from us will look on us once again. A first big step to the restoration of the family. Although this first step will not always be immediate it is the place for the healing to begin.

The hardest part of this life is living with the choices we make. We have God's forgiveness and power to love, but that's just the beginning of the race. We will still hurt and at times hurt the people we love. Our world will not be perfect, but God is in us, and we can do all things through Christ who strengthens us (Philippians 4:13).

We want all our troubles and pains to go away instantly, but remember that for every pain we have experienced we have hurt someone else. God wants to heal all the people who are on our trek through this life. He wants no one to perish; He wants all to have everlasting life (2 Peter 3:9). Jesus came to save us, and our lives returned to Him is the message of His love and forgiveness in us for them.

Were we to hurry by all the people who are a part of our life - family, friends, and even enemies - they wouldn't get to hear the love words of Jesus through us. It took a lifetime for us to fill our voids with the things of darkness. It will take a lifetime to return the full measure of God's glory and goodness to its rightful place in our hearts, minds, bodies, and souls. It takes a lifetime to rebuild a life.

Everyday affords us a time to begin again, to take another step into His good pleasure and heart of love. Along the way we carry our hearts and all that filled the void. When we dwelt in darkness we assumed to feel nothing and assumed that this all there is.

But remember, to God nothing is never nothing. He created the universe, the heavens, the earth and everyone and everything that lives here, with a word from His mouth, from nothing.

And in between the darkness and light are the man and the woman walking in the question or walking in the answer. In everyone and everything no space is unoccupied. Our Father in heaven created all things to be filled with His presence, with His goodness. His life in all things, is never ending. His love for us, for always and beyond all time. The void we presume to be is in truth a space filled with awesome blessings and wonder. It is revealed through the Son of God, Jesus Emanuel God with us. We can see through His eyes and know with His heart in the here and now and into the next.

He will show us His majesty: where we came from and where we are going and all the wonders of His love for us.

At times we may stumble in fear and maybe rebel in the face of change for moving out of our comfort zone but we can take solace in the leading of The Great Shepherd, Jesus, God with us Emanuel, our deliverer, to keep us and keep us going.

He who dwells in the secret place of the Most High, Shall abide under the shadow of the Almighty. I will say of the Lord, "He is my refuge and my fortress; My God, in Him will I trust." Surely He shall deliver you from the snare of the fowler,

And from the perilous pestilence. He shall cover you with His feathers, And under His wings you shall take refuge; His truth shall be your shield and buckler. You shall not be afraid of the terror by night Nor of the arrow that flies by day, Nor of the pestilence that walks in the darkness, Nor of the destruction that lays waste at noonday. A thousand may fall at your right hand; But it shall not come near to you. Only with your eyes shall you look, And see the reward of the wicked. Because you have made the Lord, who is my refuge, Even the Most High, your dwelling place, no evil will befall you, Nor shall any plague come near your dwelling, For He shall give His angels charge over you, To keep you in all your ways. In their hands they shall bear you up, Lest you dash your foot against a stone. (Matthew 28:18-20; Psalm 31 1-12 NKJV)

We are here at this place and time to return to our sonship and daughtership as God's children. We rebel because we are afraid of change. We should trust Jesus, the only one who can save and keep us. He has called us by His Holy Spirit.

Should you delay, certain things will occur. The apostle James wrote,

My brethren count it all joy when you fall into various trials, knowing that the testing of your faith produces patience. But let patience have its perfect work, that you may be perfect and complete lacking nothing. If any of you lacks wisdom, let him ask of God, who gives to all liberally and without reproach, and it will be given to him. But let him ask in faith nothing doubting, for he who doubts is like a wave of the sea driven and tossed by the wind. For let not that man suppose that he will receive anything from the Lord; he is a double-minded man, unstable in all his ways (James 1:2-8).

When we do not acknowledge our problems, we fall. When we see someone else fall, the personal alarms get louder until someone answers the cry. Ask while you are in the way. Emotions are always with us. They are neither good nor bad; they help us see where we are at the time. They are safety nets for us and those close to us.

Confession is good for the soul. We need to do what is righteous in all things. We have His Holy Spirit working in us, and we need each other to see where we are living together by His grace.

God's Word sternly instructs us not to harden our hearts as the children of Israel did in the wilderness. Our empowerment is not ours to possess; it is a gift of life we are to share with those in need. All we express and all the abilities we manifest are to the glory of God alone. (Ephesians 3:820).

To the chief cornerstone who is Jesus the Christ be all glory, honor, and praise. The working of the Holy Spirit of Jesus within us, gives us the power to be sons and daughters of God. As a child of God we are accountable to Him who delivers us from evil. (Matthew 6:8-13 NKJV)

The earth groans in anticipation of every man and woman in waiting for them to come to the saving knowledge of Jesus the Christ and know His love for us all. The Fathers plan of redemption for all persons born was completed when Jesus, The Holy Lamb of God died on the cross for us and with His final breath said, "It is finished.". (John 19:20)

We all start out as sons and daughters by the living fruit of our lives brought forth as husbands, wives, fathers, mothers, lovers, friends, helpers, comforters, servants; to each other. Only with faith in the Lord Jesus and by courage do we live to teach each other along the way. He will show us how to get it right if we just ask, and then wait, and then take His hand as grateful children.

Men, we are good at running away when it suits us because that's what we've been taught. We need to unlearn this response of fear. Our escape into the comfort zones in our hearts and minds lead only to a sense of futility in our souls. What good is it for us to gain the world but lose our souls? (Matthew 16:25).

In the present day and back to the 50's America changed; life really got tough and men systematically bowed out from their place as the head of the home, lover of the family and faithful sons. Many lies were given credence to; too imasculate the male person and the male role model. Because of this digression from our rightful place in our homes and in society men are just used to hiding the garage, in a bottle, or getting lost in ball game, etc..., or in a video game, hiding in fear from failure. Men we cannot run away or fade out or tune out the people that need us the most. We need to unlearn the response of fear and failure through faith in the Son of God Son of man, who knows exactly how we feel. He will show us how to get it right if we just ask and then wait and then take His hand as a grateful son. Our escape into the comfort zones in our hearts and minds is devastating to the family and leads only to futility in our soul.

What good are all the toys if we do not know the people in the next room in our own house or the one sitting right beside us? Our spouse and our children are 'unknown to us in our own home. The people we once loved have become passing shadows in the day. This is our stop sign to see where we are. The way for us in our questions of loss and pain from isolation to address our needs and give us answer for what plagues us. The answer begins with knowing where we left off in the conversation with God, the woman, and the children: with each other.

The trail to find them again can only be found in our return as sons of God through Jesus: God's only begotten Son—The Second Adam Come. He stands always waiting for us to receive His welcome once again.

He is the mystery of love from heaven come down: who came to us in the form of a baby who grew up to be a man, a son; the Savior—God with us Emanuel, Light of heaven on earth, Jesus the Christ.

Our renewed relationship with our heavenly Father is exclusively and completely through the Son of God Jesus the Christ.

When we turn to each other and give honor to Jesus by putting Him at the center of our lives, hearts, and minds, we become anchors for our families, which in turn become anchors for the world around us. Our families become refuges for others in a dark world.

If we embrace God's plan for us and our families, fear that once held us captive will be replaced by perfect love that casts out all our fear. (1 John 4:8).

We walk by faith, not by sight (2 Corinthians 5:7). The Way to walk by faith is to be a good hearer of the word of God (John 10:27) and follow Jesus, the Living Word. (Hebrews 4: 11).

We need to cast off the old things in us so we may become the new creations God has planned for us in the moment and for the rest of our lives. In all things, our heavenly Father wants us to be complete and eternally established. If we go with what we know, it will be a very short trip; we have all fallen short of the glory of God (Romans 3:23). But if we let someone bigger, stronger, and smarter carry us to the other side, we will be victors over all things.

It does matter whom you know when it comes to matters of authority. Jesus sits at the right hand of the Father and calls us His friends (John 15:14-15). When Jesus comes into our hearts, the Master of the universe has set Himself in us and we live in Him.

God is our healer (Psalm 103:1-22). He is our Great Provider (Psalm 23:1-6) and deliverer. He alone can save (Psalm 40: I-1 7). He is so much more than we could imagine or ask. He is the I AM. (Matthew 28:20).

From Genesis to Revelation, Jesus, our God and Savior, bore so many names that if they were written, the universe would not have enough space to write them. I share with you just a few to bring comfort of His promises,

- * Door (John 10: 7)
(John 14:6)
    Light of the World (John l: 1-14)
    God with 'us (Matthew 1:23)
    Prince of Peace (Isaiah 9:6)
    Lord of Lords (l Timothy 6: 15)
    King of Kings (Matthew 27:37)
    The Truth (John 14:6)
    The Life (John 1:4)
    Son of God and Son of man (Daniel 7:13-14)
    Second Adam (1 Corinthians 15:47)

- * Everlasting
Father (Isaiah 9:6) *
Savior (Luke 2: I l)

* Great Shepherd (1 Peter 5:4) only begotten Son of God (John 1:18; Psalm 2: 7 -12)
* Alpha and Omega (Revelation 21:6) * Redeemer (Psalm 130:1-8, 78:35)
Almighty God (Psalm 91: 1) * Lamb of God (John 1:29)

He is the Door because no one can come to the Father but through Him. He is the Way, for He is our breath, life and hope. He is the Light of the World come down as heaven's glory. He is the Prince of Peace, for in Him all will find rest and peace. He is Lord of Lords and King of Kings for He is over all the principalities and powers of darkness and all of heaven. He is the Truth that exposes all that has, been, is, and will be.

He is the Life our very breath that we breathe. He is the Son of God and Son of man that He could suffer with us that we would know we are never alone. He is the Second Adam that came to restore us to sonship and daughtership with the Father just as we had been in the garden of paradise. He is the Everlasting Father, for He and the heavenly Father are one. He is the Savior of the world, for He overcame all sin, death, and shame in us so we could be called sons and daughters of the Living God.

We can know hope and peace in this world in Jesus our Savior. Those who fear do so because that was all they learned. The young man's and woman's anger is simply a plea for someone to tell him there is hope and rest in Jesus our Savior. Our father in heaven created all things to be a part of something else; we call it an ecosystem. By heaven's definition, it is life and life more abundant.

We can go with what we know, yet what we know today may change tomorrow. We have to focus on the one who holds all our tomorrows in His hands and rest in His care.

The fear of loss is what troubles us the most. Stepping out in faith and trusting God to supply all our needs is a huge step. We will all fall for many reasons. And sometimes, unless we fall, we cannot advance. We continually stand at the edge of decision. We just need the right motivation to get us moving forward. We should seek God's love and forgiveness; His joy is our strength. Realizing the pleasure He takes in us helps us carry on.

He is our Redeemer for all we did against heaven; all creation has been forgiven by His sacrifice on the cross with His shed blood. He is almighty God; He rules and reigns forever and sits at the right hand of the Father. He is the Lamb of God, the perfect one in whom all things are made complete. He is love. He knows our names.

He is all we need to know.

CHAPTER 2

How Did We Let Things Get So Bad?

America began with a few people looking for something better than what they had. They represented the founding fathers and all; it was a concept, a dream of men and women brave enough to take a step of faith into the unknown.

The earliest Americans may have arrived by the Ice Bridge, which is now marked as the Bering Straits, or by inner tube while on holiday. We don't know for sure, that part of North American Continental history has been lost. Yet the story of how America began is as important to the rest of the story as the rest of the story is to the rest of the story. In truth and reality several thousand years ago a great indigenous people thrived on this continent, this America, and were the reception committee for all others who came seeking something better. They found it, the American dream, and made a life here.

This led to a great many changes for the indigenous people and the newcomers alike. The dream of America was and is God's making and His legacy. A truth that we need to keep before us. I know in part how America began and how it will end and to whom all things shall return. It is the "in betweens" that are bit sketchy due to the unknowns of our choices, age and our times. I just know that we are still here waiting to decide who we will be as a people.

As for our original most gracious hosts they are all mostly gone, the trail of tears a memorium to their plight. As for the newcomers come from the east and the other side of the west; they made their mark upon the shorelines and wonderous interior to tell of their own part in the American dream.

The American Indian nation did not fare so well because of the diseases brought with the newcomers, the remenant tribes still remain the story of the heritage of a great people who were but are no more as in ages passed. The American dream waits to see who we will be as a people who are no people at all. For as it is today we have lost sight of the vision of America as it was intended to be, losing each other along the way to something far worse. God waits for us to turn back to Him and to turn and find each other.

In the pursuit of something better, the cost of freedom has been higher than most care to admit. Freedom isn't free. The big question is, "How did we let things get so bad?" The next statement will sting a lot. The feminization of the manly man has been a root cause of the breakdown of the family in this nation and the whole world. The "Let the woman do it" attitude has caused much damage. It has allowed the devil in the door of every house and let them emasculate men. Restoring the masculine man back to his rightful place of leadership in the family is the beginning of healing for this nation and all people.

To redeem the family to its shining glory, all men need to draw the line at the door of their heart and home and say, "No more!" Thieves should steal no more (Ephesians 4:28).

The answer to the great question of how we let things get so bad will sting even more and cost us men things that we thought were so precious but are not. All those things we put between us and God and the family have got to go. Things do not make our life complete, people do. The people who love you: wife, and children and family are blessings to us, this nation, and the world. Turn to your family again, see their faces. Look into their eyes. Kneel before Jesus and let Him into your heart. This is the first step toward healing your heart and the people you are called to love.

The wife will step in to do something if the husband does not and the result will show the holes in the man that is left, in the keeping of the family. It is the man who should take the lead for things to work at, their very best, in whatever capacity he is able. The results are quite heart rending when God's chain of command is broken. The man is called to lead in love and the wife a helper to keep the conversation going and the children to be a reflection of the love learned from them. To re-enforce the family the wife is commanded to respectfully submit to her own husband. The man is commanded to devotedly love his wife as Christ loves the church and gave His life for it. These commandments are prerequisite to keeping the family strong and happy. Ultimately we need to pay heed to the two greatest commandments; Love the Lord your God with all your heart, all your mind, all your strength and all your soul and the second love your neighbor as yourself.

With this first step of surrender to what is right and good for the healing of your soul and the family, you can begin again to accept help and can enjoy the company of wife and the children and family; with a shared welcome. We need to earnestly understand the severity of the need for us to be there, to take courage for the repercussions of our neglect keep coming.

The marital commandments have been a sore spot ever since the first man and the woman's fall to sin death and shame. We are called as they were to love each other first and last and everything in between. Whatever life may throw at us, our first defense is to surrender to love and to each other in love.

Remember the treasured people God blessed you with. Look into their eyes again and again and see their heart and know their need. In the moment start the journey back to them. Take care, you may see just how far away they are from you. But don't lose heart to see the family you have created. Instead look at them through the eyes of Jesus your Savior. Love them through His heart and see the family God has redeemed back to you.

Our days are quick to pass; they are shadows. You have right now. What are you going to do with the moment? The miracle of God's love will always be there for you. God will never leave you nor forsake you (Hebrews 13:5). He will lead you out in your going out and coming in all you do (Psalm 121 : 1-8). Your Father in heaven will bless you one moment at a time.

Don't wait for your wife and children to come to you; go to them now and remind them how very important and precious they are to you. Tell them you love them. Tell them again. Then show it day by day, moment by moment.

You put all your heart and sweat into securing a living for them. Put the same effort into living with them and show them you love them. Speak God's Word to them and over them, Speak it in your house.

Speak it to their day and your day. Speak it to all the world through prayer and singing, even if you can't carry a tune in a bucket. Proclaim God's love over all you do. Remember that you never ever do anything alone. Jesus the Great Shepherd and the Father in heaven and His Holy Spirit are working for you and within you, and through you in everything you do, every step of the way.

He was there when you were conceived (Psalm 139:1-18). He will be there to meet you at your last breath and gather you to be with Him for all eternity (Matthew 28:2()). All things came from Him, and all things shall return to Him (Genesis 1 : 1-29; I Peter 4:5). He will be with you in your times of failure and triumph. He waits for you to turn to Him, so do so daily.

Men, we are anchors for our families. Stay focused on what's before you and rest in God's awesome presence and stand. When you're anticipating basketball or hockey playoffs and cheering with the crowd, listen carefully to the voices of those you should be hearing, those of your loved ones, those who want to love you. And hear your Father's call to love Him by loving them. Serve Him by submitting to His love, loving others, and being loved. Measure your days by the kindness and goodness you and your wife and children have discovered together while making memories to live by.

Empower them by teaching them to show love and receive it. The love and loving ways will return to you when you least expect it and particularly when you are downcast and fallen and need it. They are God's arms of love for you. Let them do what they are called to do, to serve you in your moment of need. In anticipation of this giant leap, take a deep breath and relax.

As men, we are stereotypically supposed to fix everything that breaks. That alone puts a lot of pressure on us. The truth is that we can't fix anything and make it good; only God can do that. So put that heavy load off your shoulders and put it where it belongs on the one who carries you and your family. Let Him lead you in the rebuilding of your loved ones.

We live in a broken world. When the first man and woman fell to sin, darkness, and shame, everything in creation was broken. But God already knew ahead of time and was already on the job. He had a plan before the words "Because I was naked and afraid" were spoken.

We aren't God; we're sons of God through Jesus. We don't have to fix everything. We just go to the Fixer and let Him fix us and our wife and children and the world around us.

There's enough grace and salvation for all who ask for all eternity. His mercy abounds toward us. How do we know this? Men, read the instruction manual, the Bible. Every tool, nut, bolt, tape measure, and anything else you need to know is all in it. And if you don't understand anything, just ask the Holy Spirit; He will empower you to be complete in all things.

God is a present help in time of need (Psalm 46:1). He made you. He knows you. He knows what you need even before you ask Him for it (Ephesians 3:20). Trust Him who saves and keeps. Call on Jesus as darkness crowds around you. Every knee shall bow and every tongue will confess that Jesus Christ is Lord (Romans 14:11). The same Jesus who overcame sin and death; He is the one that lives in you (1 John 5:1-5).

The concept of places and things changes as the Holy Spirit of Jesus reveals how heaven looks at life on earth. Everything and every person who moves around us takes on a different persona. Home is where your heart is. You can buy a house, but it doesn't become a home until you put love in it. Your home is your refuge from the world's bustle. But there is an urgency within - the remembrance of what family is all about. A cornucopia of little things that make life worth living. The sum of the parts of our life are wrapped up in the small things we do and say every day that are God's blessings to keep our days and times real.

I used to deliver food at the Lockwood mental health unit in Petoskey, Michigan. It was a unique place. Maggie, a shelter cat, lived there and comforted the people who came to the facility for rest and consolation. I met the fat cat, and we got on quite well as cats and humans go.

At the entrance of the care unit was a banner of hope to all who came and went and worked there. It was a small sign that read, "I wish for you a day full of small miracles.". In spite of all the brokenness and heartache in this life, God's small miracles help us get through. Life rarely turns out the way we planned, but those were our plans. God's plans are much better.

Unless we become like children, we cannot enter the kingdom (Luke 18:16). Our rights to sonship and daughtership begin with simply being children of God. Apart from our heavenly Father, we are helpless, hopeless, bedraggled, abandoned orphans.

We can do nothing without God's help (John 15:1-5, 5:30). If we do what our heavenly Father tells us to, our wives and children will be blessed beyond all imagination; our blessings will be pressed down, shaken together, and running over (Luke 6:38). Let us do what God said we should: "Be still and know that HE is God" (Psalm 46: 10).

The woman is soft in all the right places: heart and body and strong in mind. The man is the rock of perseverance. God has ordered us to be called to gentleness and peace. The man and the woman just need to put everything back the way it was when we started in the garden through repentance from sin and submission to each other.

Life has no pause button. It goes on whether you are with your family or they are waiting for you to show up. Your family will develop on their own if you are not there to help them do so. They love you, but you might have lost them on the way. The only way to find forgiveness is to realize a breach between you and your wife and children exists. But God's grace will allow you to patch that breach. Discover when the break occurred and start over from there together while there is yet time. Life is too short to let wounds fester.

The walk of faith in Jesus is a step in your moment. You decide how things are going to turn out. So decide. There isn't really any true accident. Such a concept is a human myth. Everything that occurs happens for a reason and from a cause. We sow things in our lives and reap what we sow, but God's grace will be with us through all the sowing and reaping and will forgive our sins.

We cannot take anything for granted; second chances are miracles that happen in God's time. In God's plan for our lives is an accountability factor we will be held to. God's plan for us is not random or something we can ignore. With every act of disobedience, we create a hurt for ourselves and whoever was with us at the time. Minimize the damage. Take time to listen to your Father and rest in His care.

We can't rewind or fast-forward our lives. We can't draw blood and forget about it. When we hurt someone, we also hurt ourselves. Everything we do will stay in our hearts and minds for the rest of our days. Make good memories and bring healing to your wife and children.

You need the joy of heaven in your life to bring His joy on earth to your house and your world. There is only one way to find it; spend time with your Father. If you want to be great, make someone greater. Take time to make the trip worth taking. You will find many good things on the way there. The real trophies for your wall of achievement are the things you built to last in the hearts of your wife and children and those who have crossed your path. Take time to hear what they say. You will motivate them to succeed in life and achieve happiness. Your loved ones will be more able to make it through the chaos of this world and be step by step closer to the love, peace, and joy of heaven's awesome company.

They will set a course of meaningful days with you and share the victorious life God wants you to have. As a bonus, you and your family will be equipped to lead other families to hear the love words of our heavenly Father. Don't think about how much time you invest; don't think about what you would rather be doing. Your time is God's time. God will bless you for loving your wife and children and all whom God sends your way.

It takes hard work to love someone. What you say and do matters more than you can comprehend. Listen to your wife. Listen to your children. Listen to the world around you. Above all, hear your Father's voice through it all.

He is everywhere you are, everywhere you have been, and everywhere you will go. Your step of faith is found in Him from this very second to eternity. There is a game plan we can go by, men.

It is all in the truth of how God does everything. God is good, so whatever He does is good. Do good with faith by your calling as a son of God.

Rejoice in the Lord always and again I say rejoice. Let your gentleness be known to all men, The Lord is at hand. Be anxious for nothing, but in everything by prayer and supplication, with thanksgiving, let your requests be made known to God which surpasses all understanding, will guard your hearts and minds through Christ Jesus. Finally brethren whatever things are just, whatever things are pure, whatever things are lovely, whatever things are of good report, if there is any virtue and if there is anything praiseworthy - meditate on these things. (Philippians 4:4-9 NKJV)

This will get you on the way to where you need to be with the Lord, your family, and the world around you. Your family will do what they see you doing and hear what you are saying. Just do what God says to do and say what God says to say. Obey Him through the power you have in Jesus as a son of God.

When you are where everything comes together through the good and bad, you are there with your wife and children as a family. You will all stand or fall together. This is your test of strength. The measure of your vitality to endure is in the character you show when you're the weakest. Who will you turn to? When you fail someone or fail at something, you are not a failure. Just remember who has your back. God will not leave you or forsake you (Hebrews 13:5).

Your wife already knows all your iniquities; you can't hide from her inquiry. Though your children do not always do what you say, they follow what you do. They know when you mess up and when you're flying right. So walk in God's forgiving love for yourself, family, friends, and even your enemies.

The Lord will resist the proud, but He also exalts the humble (Psalm 147:5-6). The one great attribute of all notable men in history is a sense of humor in their faith in the Lord Jesus and in the outcomes of their decisions. Most of what a man will do in his life will be forgotten except for his comedic remnants that will stay in people's hearts for a long time. Your wife will keep your verbal treasures tucked away in her heart to help her when the things of this life are not so funny.

The children you bring forth with your beloved wife will pass on the culture you have created by your just being yourself. The masculine image is a vital part of the foundation of the family that cannot be substituted for in any way just as the loving and caring presence of the wife is a treasure beyond all measure. I know that as men, we try to hide behind our facades, but they are all lies that keep us from being the men God created us to be.

The devil and his demons tremble at the name of Jesus for He has put all the darkness, all your enemies under your feet (James 2: 1 9; Ephesians 1:22). They know His authority over them. Walk in the authority that God has called for you walk in as a son of God. You are a light to the world in Him (John 8: 12, Ephesians 5:8).

The darkness must flee from you. The devil and the demons have to leave where the Light, Jesus, is. He lives in you. He walks in you where you walk. He's the Glory of Heaven come down to earth (John 1:14). Did I mention He's the Light of the World? Stand and give glory and praise to God (Galatians 5: l; Ephesians 6:13).

The Lord inhabits the praises of His people. His Living Word speaks in the creation of a new us. Men, our best battle plan is to completely surrender to God, our Father in heaven, and do what he says to do. Let your Savior love you. Love your wife and children just as you are loved unconditionally. Then love your neighbor next door. Keep going toward eternity and bring along those you meet along the way.

The rule of loving someone is very basic. The Lord has given to us a measure of steps of faith to meet the needs of others, and they are,

1. Look for a welcome.
2. Go to the welcome and wait for the person in his or her time.
3. Serve the one with the greatest need first nearest you.
4. If that person receives you, walk with him or her to the next person in need and serve that person.
5. If he or she does not receive you, go to the next person who will respond to your plea. Always wait for that person in his or her time, but do not give up hope in Jesus, who saves and keeps forever.

Men, your first missionary journey is to the rooms of those with whom you live; your wife, children, and anyone else living with you. God gave them to you and you to them. He knows what they need. All we can do as men is ask what they need and obey God, our Father.

We have to change our perspective if we want to clearly see what blessings we've been given and what we're to do with them. The battle is the Lord's, so don't charge in with guns blazing. Care for everyone and everything as a servant would look after his master's house. Everything you have came from the Lord, your God; it's all on loan from Him during our time on earth. Your wife has a free will, and the children you had together are the Lord's blessings you should nurture in His love. Lead by His word of promise.

Your job as a man is to be a son first and then a husband and father. You cannot hear your Father's voice unless you listen and understand what he wants from you as a son, so open your ears. It's a grow-as-you-go walk of faith. The pause doesn't have to take you to the farthest reaches of solitude. There are places and times in your life your Father has reserved for you to learn of Him right where you are. Your times and times are ordained by God every step, every deed - so listen to His voice, the Holy Spirit of Jesus, and rest in His care (Psalm 1 : 1-6).

The courage for loving and living is the answer your family waits for from you, from, your Father. To know your place as a son with the Father in heaven is the beginning of your understanding in Jesus. The walk of faith to see what your Father has for you begins now. He is not hard to find; He was always there.

CHAPTER 3

Feminine Surrender

A wise woman knows her place at the man's side. When I say this my intent is not to diminish or demean the importance of women in society or in the kingdom of God.

I simply remind us all that for things to work right, everyone needs to be where the greatest need is and be willing to meet it.

Man was created first to learn how to be a son. The woman was created from man's rib; that left him weak and vulnerable to the enemy's attack (Genesis 1:26, 2: 18-25). The woman was created from the man's rib after everything was ready for her inspiring entrance into the incredible story of love.

Anatomically, men are missing a floating rib on the left side, and women have one extra rib on the right side. Together, they comfort and cover each other with the gift of promise by grace. Any missing part of a man leaves him open to attack. A woman at his weak side is his strength, a covering to help protect him. God made us this way; with the woman covering the man's weakness, she is strong with him. It just fits like it ought to be that way.

I did not write the book, and I am not God to tell you contrary to anything that is. So with respectful candor, let us begin this journey into what being loved is all about.

We were created in God's image; God said, "Let them have dominion..." Man and woman were created to rule together as one heart and one flesh over all creation. The paradox is that the woman is called to honor the man and the man is called to woo and cherish the woman. Being in perfect step with each other, they are an unbeatable team. The power of the woman to the man is in her surrender to be loved. The power of the man is to love her as his own flesh. The woman needs to understand how to find the weak spot in the man and cover him from harm; this is revealed through prayer. It is the key strength of the family in God.

When the man falls away due to fear, that takes away the woman's power and devastates the children. Sons don't learn to give love, and daughters don't learn to receive it.

The falling away of so many men has caused panic in families since 1969, the year when everything that could attack families marched into our daily lives. That is why there has been a national emergency since then to fortify the American family. The chain of God's authority has been broken, and darkness has blinded the eyes of men and women from seeing what is good, loving and kind.

If the woman does not respect the man and the man does not love the woman, the authority of the family is trampled underfoot. All authority comes from God. When we turn from Him, we are not walking in any authority but working against all authority. The result of this destruction is a weak and fearful heart in the sons of Americans that make them unable to stand in the storm of life and our daughters losing respect for males. We can see what manner of tree these seeds of abandonment have become.

Though this discord is the by-product of a society going nowhere faster, there is some good to find out of it. A stop sign. The lesson of how things should be are screaming at us so that we cannot ignore all the terror and heartache. The voice of reason comes from an expected source - the children who have been abandoned. They're telling us what the problem is, perhaps not in the most graceful manner of communication, but they are speaking to this world that this is not right.

The man leaves the family, and the woman carries on. She is the only parental figure in the son's life, but she can't tell her son how to be a man. The son's example is absent. The son doesn't know how to respect his mother, and the mother doesn't have the right stuff to lead her son. Sonship can be passed only from father to son. The woman will try to survive, but she has lost a husband and son with the break in the family.

The beautiful thing about a woman is that she will keep going no matter how hard the road. Yet her vitality for being all she could be is lost when the husband leaves. Without him, she gets lost in the hurricane. And no matter the successes in her life, something is missing. It is that part of loving that ran away.

The son is trapped in an unnatural and unwanted situation, so he isolates himself from the mother and sisters and the rest of the family. Look at the world today and see what we have made of the family.

What I will propose will not be easy for the women of the day and may seem unfair, but the rule of loving requires us to love the one with greatest need nearest us. The first step for women to get the family back to its original glory is to see men as their allies. Taking down adversarial barriers must occur if we want to fix what has been broken.

Instead of seeing men as the cause of the hurt, please see through the eyes of love and understand we're all broken and need to get back to God's love together. Through the power of the Holy Spirit of Jesus, we can learn to forgive and get on as children of God looking through the Father's eyes of love.

Your eyes can see what God's heart sees, the man and the woman as a team. All you need to do is ask Jesus our Savior for help to understand what to do and how to help. He will answer in His powerful quiet voice without delay. He is ever watchful over us to draw us ever so near.

In the difficult area of real life, the difference between what we do and what we see and want to do and see greatly determine our getting to this other shore safely. I know you don't want to drown literally or figuratively so stop and listen to your Savior's voice, be still and know that He is God. Let Him lead you all the way through.

In reality, it will take much more to bring a man and a woman back in line with God's Word, but our way back has to start somehow, someway, some time. Now is good. It just takes a decision to accept Jesus in our hearts. He will do the rest. It all happens one step at a time.

Many discordant hearts need to be restored back to God's embrace. This will take time. Earth time. Man's time. All in God's time. With patience and perseverance we will all be a part of this miracle of His loving grace as He leads us into the moment and each day given to us as a gift of mercy. He leads us together, men and women and children and all generations into His goodness, in His time. In the present as a result of the woman breaking away from the man and the men running off and hiding, doing something they can handle without our indifference, there is a presence, a fulfillment of end time prophecy. The dominion of the spirit of the great harlot has come into open view in our daily lives. This harlot spirit dwells boldly with us, but only for a short season. As a society we have allowed her access to the family that is being dashed to pieces, for now. Her spirit lurks in overly aggressive women in open society, in the work place, in our seclusion of the dark corners of daily life. It comes through the communication devices we use without thinking a thought. We ignore what is going into our eyes and our ears, our minds and our hearts. It has infiltrated into the denominational religious groups that have a form of godliness but deny the power thereof. Her spirit is in the lies that have become part of our common speech in our culture and very thought in such a way that if you do not listen closely to discern the lies from the truth and who is talking, you will be deceived.

This Jezebel spirit, an angel of darkness, speaks in words of lust of the eyes, lust of the flesh, and in the pride of life. In our present generation pornography, the defaming of the female image, rape, and human sex trafficking is rampant in our American culture and in the cross cultures of the world. American cities, right next door to our white picket fence idealic; children, young woman, and woman of diverse ages are being bought and sold as sex slaves with the common pedestrian non the wiser. A vile evil root grows in hometown USA. Jesus said that in the last days, sin would wax worse and worse. This evil is living right next door.

But we can stop it through the power of prayer, through the power of God's love, with His Holy Spirit working with us and through us. Through repentance of sinning. Through sharing the gospel. As a society, as a whole, we must decide to put our cell phones down, look up and see the world we are living in right now. As His lights in the world we can expose this jezebel spirit and free the many people: men, women, children; from their bondage to the lust of the eyes, the lust of the flesh, and the pride of life.

Through the power of His love, Jesus the Christ the Great Shepherd, and in the power of His love for us and through us, by the power of His name the jezebel spirit will let go and move on and move out.

The jezebel spirit has been around for a while but was held back for reasons only God can say. She is here to flaunt and mock for a very short time. To understand her persona lets go back to the beginning of the ending of one story and the beginning of a new story. Once upon a time, in a beautiful garden a man and a woman were naked and unashamed and free to love each other, and were just learning how to understand this awesome love and what it meant to the one who created them and loved them first. There was a tree whose fruit God the Creator, forbade them to eat lest they eat of it and die. And it was created before the woman was created from the man's rib, everything the man knew the woman knew and they were both called— Adam, from the root word meaning red clay, for that is how the Creator God our heavenly Father formed both of them into being. They were both equal in purpose but only together. They were one in purity of holiness. And when the man joined with the woman they became one flesh, but deeper still they were one heart, the two beating with one pulse, with one heart song. And God the Creator, their heavenly Father spoke to them as one person, although they were two, as one, standing in God's authority, equal together.

One day the man walked away from the woman for just a short time and left her alone. The deceiver came and possessed a snake. The snake spoke to the woman and this was the conversation: The serpent, "Has God indeed said, you shall not eat of every tree of the garden?".

The woman, "We may eat of the fruit of the trees of the garden; but of fruit of the tree in the midst of the garden, God has said, YOU shall not eat it, nor shall you touch it lest you die.".

The serpent, "You will surely die. For God knows that in the day you eat of it your eyes will be opened and you will be like God, knowing good and evil.".

So when the woman saw that the tree was good for food, that it was pleasant to the eyes and a tree desirable to make one wise, she took of its fruit and ate. She also gave to her husband with her and he ate.

The eyes of both of them were opened and they knew they were naked; and they sewed fig leaves together and made themselves coverings (Genesis 3: 1-7).

At the turning of their hearts, all the forthcoming generations would do and replay this chain of feelings because that is the foundation of and their emotional beginnings.

But that was just the beginning of the love story of the ages. Let us finish our tale. In Genesis we read. At the moment the lust of the eyes, the lust of the flesh, and the pride of life was ushered into the lives of the man and the woman they were cut in half in the heart and mind and their bodies torn apart from each other in a most horrid way. Their eyes were opened to the lust of the flesh instead of loving each other in purity and holiness their lust for each other took them over. The power to rule together was broken and torn apart. The break of their shared trust was replaced with the lust of the eyes, the lust of the flesh, and the pride of life; sin overtook them, they died in their soul. Their covenant was broken with God, Creator and Father; and with each other because of their disobedience. The two that were one in heart, mind, and body were now two only made one in the flesh through the lust of the eyes, the lust of the flesh, and the pride of life; divided in heart, mind and authority. Sin, death and destruction put a veil of blindness between them and God and each other. They were struck blind from seeing each other in the purity of love in the beauty of His holiness.

And now for the first time they knew fear, anger, emptiness and isolation. They feared how they would get back to each other. They feared how they would get back to their relationship with God, their Creator and Father, to walk in His love and comfort, to know His peace, His joy and His rest. Because of their disobedience it cut and wounded all future generations with sin, death, destruction, and isolation. And for every person born after them this course of feelings and fear, that came from their fall to sin and death, is replayed in every part of our relationship with each other and everything apart from His love for us; which comes to us from His Son Jesus the Christ. The story of sin and death is not the end of the story. I say again, God our heavenly Father loved them and all of us first before we ever were, so let us finish with the rest of the story.

"And they heard the sound of the Lord God walking in the garden in the cool of the day, and Adam and his wife hid themselves from the presence of the Lord God among the trees of the garden."

"Then the Lord God called to Adam and said to him, "Where are you?". So he said, "I heard your voice in the garden and I was afraid because I was naked; and I hid myself.".

"And He said, "Who told you that you were naked? Have you eaten from the tree of which I commanded you that you should not eat?". Then the man said, "The woman whom You gave to me, she gave me of the tree, and I ate." And the Lord God said to the woman, "What is this that you have done?" The woman said, "The serpent deceived me and I ate.".

"So the Lord God said to the serpent: "Because you have done this you are cursed more than all cattle, And more than any beast of the field, on your belly you shall go, and you shall, eat dust all the days of your life. And I will put enmity between you and the woman and between your seed and her seed; he shall bruise your head, And you shall bruise his heel."

"To the woman He said, "I will greatly multiply your sorrow and your conception. In pain you shall bring forth children; Your desire shall be for your husband, And he shall rule over you." Then to Adam He said, "Because you have heeded the voice of your wife, and have eaten from the tree of which I commanded you, saying, "You shall not eat of it all the days of your life. Both thorns and thistles it shall bring forth for you, and you shall eat the herb of the field. In the sweat of your face you shall eat bread till you return to the ground, For out of it you were taken; For dust you are, and to dust you shall return.".

"And Adam called his wife Eve because she was the mother of all living. Also for Adam (the man) and his wife the Lord God made tunics of skins and clothed them. (It was the first promise of the Lord God's plan of redemption regarding the slain Lamb of God on the cross.)

"Then the Lord God said, "Behold the man has become one of Us, to know good and evil. And now, lest he put his hand out to take the tree of life, and eat, and live forever".- therefore the Lord God sent him out of the garden of Eden to till the ground from which he was taken. So he drove out the man; and He placed cherebim at the east of the garden of Eden, and a flaming sword which turned every way, to guard the way to the tree of life." (Genesis 3: 1-24)

But that's not the end of the story. The Lord God already had a plan of redemption to bring the man and woman back to the place of loving each other and to fellowship with Him. The plan has a name: Jesus, the only begotten Son of God, the Lamb of God.

The mark of the Jezebel spirit was made on the woman's heart. Still, love is always there to woo her back to the man and to the fellowship with the Lord God.

And so we have the tale of the two cities before us. The one of life that became us, the story of sin and death and darkness. The second, the story is of our way back to God's love and His path of righteousness where we find each other again and again. A life without fear of being loved and reaching out to love the Lord God and the woman, the children, your neighbor as yourself.

The man knows his failure. He walked away. By the Lord's strength to love again he can turn around and come back to those that love him. The woman knows where she went wrong and how life should be and through the power of God's love she can come along side of the man to begin again, without fear of being left alone, stranded in this cold uncaring world. And so the drama continuous in our journey back to walking and talking with our Father, Creator, God, Savior, dearest friend, The Great Shepherd in the moments of our day. The second story of our way back to God's love and His path of righteousness, where we are found in Him and where we find each other again and again living a life without fear of being loved and reaching out to love the Lord God, the woman, the children; our neighbor as ourselves.

We find a mystery and a promise in the apostle Paul's first letter to the Corinthians:

"Love suffers long and is kind; love does not envy; love does not parade itself, is not puffed up; does not behave rudely, does not seek its own, is not provoked, thinks no evil; does not rejoice in iniquity, but rejoices in the truth; bears all things, believes all things, hopes all things.

Love never fails. But whether there are prophecies, they will fail; whether there are tongues, they will cease, whether there is knowledge, it will vanish away.

For we know in part and prophesy in part. But when that which is perfect is come, then that which is in part will be done away.

When I was a child, I spoke as a child, I understood as a child, I thought as a child; but when I became a man I put away childish things.

For now we see in a mirror, dimly, but then face to face. Now I know in part, but then I shall know just as I am known.

And now abides faith, hope, and love, these three; but the greatest of these is love." (Corinthians 13:4-13)

The greatest power in the universe is love. It bears a face and a name above all names, Jesus the Christ. Love created this world and the stars from nothing because God saw us first. All things were created by and for love. All creation is in the presence of love. This truth we have to help guide us to being loved and loving others.

Before the breach of trust between the man and the woman, life in the garden was fair and equal, but the man and woman broke with God and made all things unequal for everybody and everything. Love isn't fair because of what love is; it gives itself away. Anything apart from that fact is confusion and leads to rabbit trails that take us nowhere. So let us stick to the subject. The sticky notes are everywhere, so the information trail is well marked.

The culture we have come to accept has allowed a gazillion lies to infiltrate our speech and thoughts that need to be identified before we can move on. They are all held within the morals and morays that we accept as everyday life. They have a name; they attach to everything and have a designation in mind - us.

There is God's plan. There is the devil's plan. And we have our plans. Following the winning plan determines if we live or die. Whom we serve and obey makes all the difference between heaven and hell. God's plan is the best one. The course we take is determined by our decisions. Therein lies the dilemma for the family in today's messed-up world. We chase after things that have nothing to do with love and good. The Jezebel spirit that took hold of the woman's heart isn't in hiding anymore; it stands in plain sight. But it's just one of the many in the audience that sees and hears everything we do and say, everything we have invited into our lives by omission. Our lives are on display for all creation to see; we can hide nothing. All we do is there for anyone who wants to watch our lives unfolding.

Reality TV didn't come up with the idea of anything goes; it's merely a reflection of what we have accepted as normal. We stand in the presence of light and truth in this generation, and we ache for something real. Why do you think we gravitate toward such things? We're already there.

God and His angels watch us from heaven, as do the powers of darkness. All creation watches us. If we think, fart, sneeze, fall or rise up, go out or come in, if we lie down; it is all illuminated for all of heaven and the dominions, and all of creation to see and hear. The light of God exposes everything we do so that we cannot hide anything, at any time. His truth will find us out in His presence. God the Creator is in all things, through all things, and above all things; as King and Lord of all—Jesus the Great Shepherd is He.

Families are healed when the man stays with the woman and the woman surrenders to the man's love. The family depends on the love the woman receives and gives and the faithfulness of the man to her.

In society, the wounds are deep and many because the man does not know his place in the woman's life and the woman has failed to cover the weak spot of the man. We are ordained by the Lord God to love each other. When we don't we clearly see the result.

This brings us to the root of the gender adversity. The woman is afraid of being unloved. The man is afraid because he doesn't feel he has the right stuff. This breeds anger, division, and discord between the two. We can be only where we are presently; where we are headed is a mystery. Love between a man and woman is a big question mark if we try to figure it out on our own. We never will as long as we hold to what we know in this flesh and blood world. Our lusts and pride blind us from seeing the beauty that love is.

It's all in the details. God's plan seems unfair to the woman because her idea of love is contrary to what love is. The woman fantasizes of a perfect husband, children, and home; that does not reflect the real world. There is no perfect husband; all men have lust issues, anger issues, and self-esteem issues; when men can't find answers, they hide; it's easier that way.

There are no perfect children. Every person's the seed of Adam's sin nature. Left to themselves, children become adults who love by the lust of the eyes, the lust of the flesh, and the pride of life.

There is no perfect home. All have leaks, breaks, messes, laundry, dishes... There is no perfect world apart from Jesus. The world and everything in, around, and under it is being renewed by Him. And it can start anew with you, right now.

The banner across the sky reads "Under Construction Watch Your Step 'Cause the Next One Is a Doozy.". Living is quite intense most of the time, and it's like anything else; if you look at something for too long without a break, you lose sight of what you're looking at. If you're seeking an answer while you struggle, you'll just wear yourself out. God gave us people to work with; a view from afar helps us see more clearly.

The man in this life needs all the help he can get just to stand and stand and stand. God gave him a "Wow" to be at his side, the woman, wrapped in his arms and doing what she does best, being loved and giving love. God made the woman to be a gift of grace and beauty to shine in the man's life. A man who has a woman who will walk with him and grow with him is blessed beyond measure.

The women of this generation are missing out on the best heaven has to offer. The clock is ticking. It's more than just being a comforter for the man it is all about what pleases our heavenly Father.

It's knowing that your heavenly Father is pleased and you can go to Him any time without the barrier of disobedience between you and heaven's company. Just ask.

The real blessing of love isn't for the moment; it's forever. True love is the stuff you just know. It will always be there no matter what. That's what the man and woman had in paradise and lost; together, the two can have it once again in God's plan of redemption. Jesus overcame the world, darkness, sin, death, fear of loss, and the grave; everything that went wrong has been made right again in obedience to Jesus.

I have learned that for the woman, it's all about knowing something. God made the woman's brain that way to help keep order in this crazy life. But there are some things God left for us to accept because it is better for the one with the greatest need. It is called faith.

Everything we want is not what we need. The best is not the best. It is what brings happiness that is the real treasure we hold in our hearts. Love will hurt a bit once in a while to get to the good stuff, but we already knew that; we just don't like it. Still, we have to follow through. Love is worth the trip.

Loving someone will take everything you have and then more of the things that we do not have. Love is the only thing that matters. It is the trail that leads the woman back to the arms of the man right where she belongs as the man stands in the loving arms of Jesus. It makes a way for the man to know love.

The belief of being loved is a powerful force in the universe. God's love. When we are loved, we gain inner strength and can clearly see who and where we are.

In the real world right now, women's anger blinds them to love when it comes softly and gently as a whisper of the heart. Without love, a woman is lost just as the man is lost without her at his side. The two can be healed if they walk together in Jesus. The power of the woman to love the man changes in the world around her and heals her heart and the man.

The light of love exposes the bad stuff and forces it out to make room for the good stuff. This gift that the woman has been given is a gift only she was created to give. God made her that way to be a blessing to the man. The gates of hell cannot prevail against her love with Jesus in it as the man and woman walk as one. And just as the woman spends her life seeking to be loved, the miracle of her heart brings peace to the home and family and to all as she walks in the power of the Lord's presence.

Much unnecessary pain follows a woman's life when she resists God's perfect plan. But God's grace will overcome that resistance. There is far too much drama in the way we want things to be and how they really are. All things of life are not serious - stuff like the bathroom wars. Seat up of seat down. Toothpaste tube squeezed at the middle, not at the end. Toilet paper hanging over or under. Who picks up all the wet towels on the floor. Who's turn is it to (fill in the blank). Humor tells the tale of us and what really matters in life. The little things we can share and carry with us wherever we go. They make loving interesting.

A man cannot think like a woman, nor can a woman think like a man, but the two together form the perfect vessel for God to fill with

His love. Man and woman need each other; their love in Him is life to heart and mind and hope for the generations in Christ.

It all hinges on surrender; the surrender of the woman to be loved by the man and the man willing to lay down his life to love and cherish her. This is God's plan; submission to God and to each other. The man covers the woman with his love, and the woman covers the weak spot of the man to comfort and protect him.

In the getting on of all the 'he said's and "she said's", love tells the story behind the story. I listen to the old tunes, and sometimes, God teaches me through what other people do when they have no idea how they would be used to reveal a truth. One song goes like this: "Beautiful love songs are never out of date. Hearts full of passion, jealousy, and hate.

Woman needs man and man must have his mate. That no one can deny.".

Man and woman need each other. They are wonderful creations God said were good. Man and woman were meant to be inseparable. They were created to grow each other. It is the gift meant to shine bright and strong in the darkness all around.

We need to see the writing in the sky, on the bathroom wall, the water tower in John Deere green, on every underpass, bridge, tree, and rock. The man and the woman were just meant to be together for the world to be right.

The marriage was never about who's who, but now that we're here, let's stay a while.

The world will tell man and woman they don't need each other to be happy and complete. This lie is a serious attack on the family as governments consider homosexuality acceptable. Countless times, God brought down pestilence on kingdoms founded on such practices. To this day, the brimstone that fell on the depraved generations is a reminder that under heaven, this is not acceptable.

Anything cannot be anything we want to make it, God created everything and said it was good. Be assured that God will not be mocked.

For us He has created something beautiful, wonderful, awesome; the family which bears His seal of approval, a man, a woman, and children to bless their house, to bless the Lord our God and Father. The blessing being kept in the man loving the woman, the woman surrendering to the man's love, and the children following in the loving way of the lessons they have learned, to continue the work of God—to believe in the one whom God sent, Jesus the Christ, the Messiah come, God with us—Emanuel.

Through Christ, the love that once was is returning to the man and woman one little miracle at a time, step by step, back to each other. Love has always and will always be. By faith, the man and the woman will have paradise once more through God's grace as the two walk in obedience to God's command, to love one another as He loves us completely.

Every day is a time to find each other once again to make love new by His calling and power as His own through His Spirit of love. A life of submission is for all to bear. It is proof we are Christians by our love.

Love through faith, be loved by faith, and know how much you are loved forever.

CHAPTER 4

I Know Why Young Men Rage

"In the last days men's hearts will fail for fear" (Luke 21 :26 NKJV). I write this as an introduction because it exemplifies the state of our society right now. We are living in the end times. Whether people believe in Jesus and His salvation through His shed blood on the cross or if people have yet to hear and understand, everybody knows that there is a cataclysmic change the world. Something very big is happening. Also everybody knows deep down that there is nowhere to hide from whatever is coming. The paradox of here and now is that God is our refuge and it is God who comes to bring His judgment on the earth to dot all the "i's" and cross all the "t's" in the story of redemption of man and woman.

The young men and young women feel the change along with all of creation and tremble for fear, someone needs to "eye ball to eye ball", tell them and show them the words of life and hope; the words of Jesus the Christ our Savior. They need the foundation of community to draw strength from. Community begins in the company of God our Father through His Son Jesus.

In a recent poll taken about a decade ago, people, the ages of thirteen through twenty six were asked one question, "What is the most important thing that matters to them.".

With the world literally at their fingertips the most common answer was time with family. We live in the age of hyper speed of communication devises that allows us the ease and access to talk to anyone anywhere in nano seconds through Skype, texting and whatever is being constructed in the very next minute. In society today the family is comprised of a tiny little box with even smaller buttons that people cling to with their very life's breath. There is no human connection. The relationship of human contact is gone in so much of our life. The accelerated change in the way we talk to each other is moving so fast that our hearts and our minds cannot keep the pace. In the real world God created our minds and our hearts to require highs and lows and pauses in between, a routine and a time rest, a time to stop and see where we are and where we are going and who is walking with us. Technology is a great tool, but it is only a machine, not a person. It does not offer us love or hope. It does not give us peace. We cannot exist in a life compressed by virtually reality. We do not live in nano seconds. We live in the moments and hours of a very short time on this earth. A time given for our return back to our heavenly Father's side. Our little POOF! is all the time we have to return to God's wonderful, awesome fellowship.

This generation needs to know that there is so much more to this life that can only be found when we are rejoined with our heavenly Father and with each other in holy and righteous fellowship. The older generations is also lost in the gadgets of our day, just floundering in entitlement and ease while the younger generation look on wondering who will lead them into what is right and what is good. The young are so devastated by the lack of human leadership and human relationship and the loss of faith in love and hope that suicide is sadly common place and a growing trend of a way out of the madness in a society gone wrong. With the break of the family and quite literally the family redefined by evil intent, it has left everything in doubt. The rage in this generations hearts and minds is justified and rightfully requires an answer. God our Father in heaven has given us the command to love Him with all that we are and to love each other as ourselves in service to one another. We are all accountable.

When children are left to themselves with just the lust of the eyes, the lust of the flesh and the pride of life unchecked, the hopelessness of life grows around them as a great cloud of darkness, pressing their very life's breath out of them. Walking in this overwhelming fear they are even more blinded by their anger. The anger turned to rage is the state of the young mind today. Society treats the young rebel as the problem. In truth they are the symptom of what we have allowed to be with a society of neglect. We are reaping what we have sown.

The state of the mindset of the young men and women is the evidence of the lack of elder leadership. Which exposes an even greater lack. The older generation do not know how to lead the younger generation back to stability. In far too many religious sects it is the women who lead with the man fearful of failure, stepping aside of their God given calling.

As a result of the failings of the older generation males the resentment towards women has become a social pandemic of abuse, rape, horrific violence, with the woman, with all women, as targets of male aggression. A clear sign of the chaos we have accepted as normal behavior,

We have a plan, our plan, to pacify the problem through education, counseling, drugs and therapies that are all based on our assumptions of falsehood. But that is our plan. A plan without God's direction. Without His power to change the heart, apart from the Lord and Savior Jesus, The Great Shepherd, is no plan at all. Only God's love in us and working through us can resolve the hatred and resentment, and fear to smother the rage of men against women. The family can only return as a family when we let love and let God. The young men need to be led into sonship; to understand what being a son is, how to be a manly man. Our society keeps trying to press them into a mold that doesn't fit them. Their souls are rebelling tearing away at anything that remotely resembles authority over them. What we have accepted as being a community has become just a revolving door. A return back to the fifties, sixties, and the seventies.

Regardless of the hurt young men feel, they have no right to harm, degrade, or humiliate any woman. Enough is enough; it's time for a change for the good, to become the family we are called to be by God's design. The family needs to be a family. Fathers need to be fathers. Mothers need to be mothers. Children need to be allowed to be children without the weight of the world on their shoulders.

The lies of this world have brought much harm to the male image. Where are the examples of caring male leaders? They are the fathers, grandfathers, and uncles.

Males need to stand up, stand in, and step up to make our way back to our place of leadership in God's ordained role as sons, husbands, fathers and brothers. The trust between males must be restored to its glory in our Father in heaven. A healing of the male image in the church of America is necessary now!

The only way for a son to be a son is to do what his father is doing and say what his father says in like manner to women and each other. It's our responsibility as male role models to honor our Father by obeying His commandments and love each other in peace and unity.

We have God's word to read and learn from. Jesus has given us His Holy Spirit to empower us to be sons of God. It is time now to become males who please our Father in heaven and be the example that younger men need; that all men need. They need us to be what we are called to be so they can get on with living and loving. Authority isn't genetic; it has to be learned. The relationship between father and son and man and man is the only vehicle God has given us to pass it on.

This accountability to God and our fellow men cannot be put off for the next generation to pick up because we are the next generation. If we don't lead our sons into manhood, they won't know how to achieve manhood. The hour of our decision to make a change, is here now. The breakdown of the family is painfully obvious. God's plan is all laid out for us. It's our time to be men!

Now is the time to make a difference in the lives of those we are called to love. For the sake of all men everywhere, the road back to wholeness starts with a look in the mirror and an assessment of the man we are. Are we the man God has called us to be? Let us see where we are right now so we can get on for the sake of others who are depending on us into leading them to manhood. Only a man can show a son how to be a son by being one himself. Take the time to ask Jesus, the Great Shepherd how to walk, how to talk, how to work, how to love, how to welcome others.

We men are held by our memories until we learn to get past them and move on. We cannot go forward until everything has moved forward with us. We can be sons of God through the Holy Spirit. This promise is found in gospel according to John the beloved:

"He was in the world, and the world was made through Him, and the world did not know Him. He came to His own, and His own did not receive Him. But as many as received Him, to them He gave the right to become children of God, to those who believed in His name; who were born, not of blood, nor of the will of the flesh, nor of the will of man, but of God." (John 1:10-13).

The power is given to us through Jesus Christ living in us by His Holy Spirit, but we can learn to be sons only by doing what He does when we see Him do it. Jesus said:

"I am the vine and you are the branches. He who abides in Me, and I in Him, bears much fruit; for without Me you can do nothing. If anyone does not abide in Me, he is cast out as a branch and is withered; and they gather them and throw them into the fire, and they are burned. If you abide in Me, and My words abide in you, you will ask what you desire, and it shall be done for you. By this My Father is glorified, that you bear much fruit; so that you will be My disciples." (John 15:5-8).

We must be sons in the likeness of the Son to lead others into the truth of becoming sons of God through the power of Christ's Spirit. We must take up our cross and follow Him to see what He does so we can show other men how to be sons and live life more abundantly and in peace.

The young men of this generation are watching and waiting for us older men to get it together so they can see what real men look and act like. A boy doesn't become a man by accident or by mere survival of the fittest. A male can be born, but the man he is called to become is built one day, one heart rending moment at a time. Someone has to be there to meet him on the path to manhood. That someone is us.

If we want the world to be right, we need to acknowledge the fact that we have let the role of mentor fall away like the ashes scattered in the wind. Young men are lost because no one has told them what life is all about. Society offers them nightmares without any hope, peace of mind, of stability of the family. Who will tell them rightly if we do not? They will seek answers elsewhere if we do not tell them. The powers of darkness are waiting in the wings to lead them into helplessness and hopelessness if we do not take the lead by God's direction.

If we are the sons of God empowered by the Holy Spirit of Jesus, we must imitate Jesus as He does what the Father in heaven does. As we walk with Jesus doing what he does, men of all ages will see and follow. What they look for is someone real. In this day of falsehood, true men are hard to find.

Men of strength of character are difficult to see because true integrity and honor for family and goodness are not as common as they once were. Make it matter today.

Young men are treated like trees in a forest. No one sees their faces, learns their names, or wonders what's in their hearts. We think a holiday event is enough to meet the needs of people's souls. We live in the trenches with young men, but we don't see them in the darkness.

They are terrified of the doubt and the neglect they have lived through. They have had all that they can tolerate of everything being wrong. They are angry because the majority of our society does not even notice that there's something wrong with them and that the destruction of our country and world is at hand. The trust they need to know is profaned by politicians who make dangerous decisions for the country the young will have to live with.

The young men of this generation want what is right and good and to know the security of the family (father, mother, brother and sisters), and a normal life in a normal world in which men are men and women are women and a kid can be a kid. They need to hear words of affirmation from real men, words everybody needs to hear, the words of life, hope, peace and rest.

If you really want to learn why so many young men are so angry, unplug your ears and hear all the lies the world is telling us. Notice how we ignore even the basic amenities of human decency toward each other daily.

They hurt because we all hurt, hurting each other. Without a guide to walk with and talk with, face to face all they have is a panic button. Their finger is pressing hard, but apparently their cries of pain are not loud enough for us to hear to reach our dulled sense of hearing. How much worse does life have to get for our American society to get a clue, to notice, that we are being burned alive by our lust and greed?

Now is the time for us to draw near to our Father in heaven as He calls for us to do. We can't hear until everyone stops and acknowledges where we are and how bad things have become. We have neglected and mocked the good things God has given us.

It's not right for our young men to be violent, but this is the real world, where push comes to shove, and they have been pushed too far. They are the fruit of the seeds we have sown. It is time to bring redemption to this generation and get real about relationship with our heavenly Father. It is long past time that we get real with the hurt we are causing by letting our wound fester. We need to profess with our mouth and believe in our heart that there is hope in Jesus our Savior, so that those we are called to love, will know the way to find rest at the feet of Jesus the Great Shepherd, God with us Emanuel. That we may know how to be sons and daughters of God. There is no middle ground for the hurting: there is despair and there is liberty. To know the liberty of living, to know rest, His rest, is to stop and kneel or fall at the feet of Jesus the Christ and surrender to Him alone.

You can't fake it. Don't bother opening your mouth until you have His words of love to share. You will be known by the fruit you bear, and young men will see you as a fake if you try to live a lie. If you want to know what kind of fruit a tree bears, just look at the tree. What manner of tree are you? When a troubled, seeking soul inquires of you the words of life, do you have them to give? If we follow Jesus, we will be a tree of good fruit with the words of life that all will recognize His good in us. If we say we follow Jesus but in truth follow our own way, the fruit we bear will make a stink in the lives of other. The fruit of today's denominations gives off a foul odor and has made the church weep in sorrow.

The people of this generation know what is right and good for us all because of the alarm that is going off inside their hearts to warn them of the time that is quickly running out. They need answers. They need to hear the words of life from you. They can only hear if someone speaks the words into their ear. The words of forgiveness and the awesome love that God has for them. We are all accountable to share this good news. We are his hands and feet; the body of Christ.

We have been warned by Jesus in John 15:5-8 of what will happen if we do not love God and each other and follow Him by living by His Spirit in us. The body of Christ is called to walk in unity as Jesus is one with the Father in Spirit and in truth. We have an entire generation of young people who are isolated, afraid, and hopeless.

We are called to live the truth in love and deed (Colossians 3:12-17). We are to remember that we are not above or apart from correction from anyone in the body of Christ; no one is exempt from reproof, exhortation, or instruction in the truth. We are all commanded to submit ourselves one to another for we are all the body of Christ. The whole body is affected by whatever happens to any one of its parts (2 Timothy 3:1-17; I Corinthians 12: 12; Romans 12:14). Our primary purpose in the body of Christ is to lead others to be found in Jesus our Lord and Savior.

Twenty years ago, I wrote an inspiring essay for the Alpena News regarding the role of community and how important it is to establish a strong society. What I wrote is true even more so today.

What Is Community?

Of all society's grandest ponderings is the question, What Is Community?

The deepest sense of my searching here in this life is not nor has been, how much I could get from others and this world but rather where is my place.

I listened long and quiet and from the mind of a sage came the answer for which I long sought for. It was not the answer to the mysteries of the universe. It was comprised of one single thought - community.

The grandest wealth a person has is their sense of being founded upon, of, and with their community, in the truth.

Community? Is it the premise of morays and morals based upon our family and friends, or is it more than that. Likened unto our eternal journey and the people than become the pathways and highways that help us become who we are, in Christ'?

Much has happened to me and death has knocked on my door a few times, as I think about it, it is by His grace that I live today to tell the story that there is so much more to community that what is seen by our physical eyes.

The greatest treasure of my life came to me, when I had become, in Jesus our Savior.

For I was given an answer to the great question of life, "To be or not to be?", and the answer that was given to me was, "I AM". He knows my name and He has called me to walk with Him.

It is the incorruptible gem of kings and common people.

To be is to be His! It is the one and only thing that makes us all equal and all the same in purpose, place of honor and love; in essence of truth - community.

The hardest times of life are when we feel all alone, in times of tragedy, and yet, it is during those times, at that stopping place, where we can find our sense of purpose, our center of being. For that is when the hand of love reaches out to us. It shall ever remain a place of remembrance. For to be is as much a time as it is a place, when we, as community, give the sense of purpose, a face with hands and feet with strong arms extended to embrace and support the one in need, to share an eternal moment to complete the circle of community's function.

Community is not just a word, it is a promise of great expanse that knows no boundaries, of geography, nationality, or state of physical stature or chronological placement.

Like a two edged sword, love of community cuts away the darkness, to let the light of hope shine, despite the erring wanton ill of humanity. And it adheres the giver and the taker in the precise moment of the sharing, in the act of giving so that no one escapes without leaving something behind them, for the good.

Community is the eternal being, God our Father, reflected in all persons, giving each one the sense, "To Be.", to know the treasure of life, the gem, priceless and attainable, by the one who is the PERFECT SON JESUS, and found by all who may come.

Community, is not so much a matter of a question, it is more a matter of an answer.

When the answer bears a face and has a name the gem is found, life is JESUS THE SON OF GOD.

Community, an answer, a journeys end, which is called home, in Him. And the home of which I speak has not beams of wood or made of stone or steel, but rather it is vibrant strands of rainbows, tickles, and hugs that breath us. Thereby, we not only become to be, but all the more we are His breath in motion, a tiny candle glow, that when finding our place, we are light of heaven on earth in Him.

And of the candle glow there are tumults of person's born, and person's passed on, and person' s not yet born, being breathed by eternities glow of wonder, the light of heaven, JESUS. And there of the glow, each person's face shining pure and soft, stands a doorway, loves mystery unfolding, giving place for all "To be! " where I AM smiles and welcomes, with open arms, for the weary traveler, giving them the gift of peace of mind and body, to give them, all who may come, a place to rest forever in the sharing of His words of life.

Community is where we dream, where we are born into His light and where we die.

It is Him in us. And we are on the gateway to hopes end, for home is where the heart is.

And the heart is God's place to be in us. God being in us, we shine the gift of the All-In-One, extending the invitation to all person's born, to come, "To be!" For each one that is born, that dreams, and hopes, and breaths, is precious. We are all a gift of hope and love, a home in which friend's dwell, as we walk in His love.

And there being home, wrapped in the embrace of His love, in us and all around us, the journey finds the answer to the question, "What is community?".

And concluding gently, the answer is stated freely, that the treasure of community is not in the one that is sought, but instead it is the one who is found.

And the truth in purest hope and love, this indeed is community.".

Being found is what we all long for. We want to be heard, seen, and acknowledged as a part of the bigger picture. We want to know we are part of eternal life of heaven on earth. Young men and women lack the two most important things: a relationship with God our heavenly Father and each other. The relationships can only be found in walking and talking with Jesus our Savior God with us and being found in the wonder of a caring community.

The sons of God are called to speak words of hope and life to the sons of men. The young men and young women during these end times look at you and me to hear the words of our Father, the words of life. They seek peace of mind and heart and rest for the body and soul.

We are the body of Christ. We are His hands and feet. Young men and women today are declared by God's heart of love, our destination. The journey into redemption and fellowship awaits us, and it begins for you and me today. It is for His love's sake that we go to the young men who rage in fear and pain. They ask, "Does anybody hear me?".

The young men and women who are fearful of being loved in truth and holiness are asking, "Does anybody see me? Does anybody care?".

Our Father in heaven has heard their cries, and we are to give them an answer, God wants them to be set free. We are called to answer their cry that they may come to be in Jesus' name.

CHAPTER 5

It's All In The Voice You Hear

The human ear is a powerful gateway to the heart, mind, and soul. We hear by God's design as indicated in the apostle Paul's letter to the Romans: "So then faith comes by hearing, and hearing by the word of God. But I say have they not heard? Yes indeed: Their sound has gone out to all the earth. And their word to the ends of the world" (Romans 10:17-18 NKJV).

What people tell us, what we hear, and how we hear are the foundation of the memories, the bits and pieces of life, and love and loss and gain.

The mystery of God's wondrous lullabies fills the air and our senses. We hear and know the incredible miracle of sound as it unfolds all around us. Creation is God's symphony in the key of extra awesome. Sound and matter are the confirmation of time and space. Physical objects take shape in our minds when we hear a thing or a person. Just by the sound they make, we can know where they are, who they are, and exactly what they are doing at that moment; it paints a picture in our memories.

Our minds and hearts hear; as we listen, our knowledge of whomever and whatever gives us direction is imprinted in our thoughts. When we hear waves crashing, we know we're by a lake or sea. Spring winds sound different from autumn blasts. Trees in bloom herald the coming of spring. In the fall, the notes they strum speak surrender to the coming winter. The footsteps of people tell their own tales with the rise and fall of heel and toe.

When we close our eyes and even when we plug our ears creation around us speaks even more fluently; the sounds of silence. We shall ever remain a part of the melodies and harmony that resounds in the heavens time and beat, as sure as the voice of God dances in every space between the spaces.

Did you ever wonder what the difference is between one note and another? Space. God used the one note of His heart to bring the beauty of His holy, pure voice into our ears. It is a note of His majesty and wonder.

Life is the music of God's heart in constant motion; all we need to do is pause to hear Him everywhere. As our lives play out all creation, the physical and spiritual worlds are our constant audiences. There is no place we can hide because God wants us to always be found.

As the notes play, dance, and sing in this miracle of sounds, his desire is fulfilled. He wants all creation to hear Him no matter where we are.

"Let everything that has breath praise the Lord" (Psalm 150:8 NKJV). What is this everything that has breath?". Everything God made to live and move. We inhale. We exhale. And in between, there is a pause in anticipation of the next one. The pause is to bring us back to our Creator God and know it is His breath in us. His life. His time and times. This is beginning point of understanding that He is the source of all life. All things created live in Him.

Not one thing God has made is excluded from His song; it is the echo of love in response to all He has done. The space between each note is the mystery we can only marvel at. We can explain it away as wavelengths that separate one note from another, but what is in the wavelength itself? What fills the distance from here to there? In the breakdown of the musical scales is a trail of algorithms God put in place for us to hear His songs of love for us.

The science of sound is fascinating, but it's the majesty of it all that gives us the overwhelming pause in the hearing of it all.

In the basic scale of musical tones is the range of what humans, cats, fleas, giraffes, and gnus and gnees can hear. We call it megahertz, but that doesn't define what the ranges of sound really are. This hypothesis raises more questions. The answer is God's love. God's plan. We cannot grasp the sound of the speed of thought or the tones of angels in flight. Deep in the ocean are creatures whose songs to God we may never hear. There are sounds we cannot comprehend but only appreciate and be in awe and wonder of. Everything that has breath has a voice. We need to stop and understand that all life was created by God and for His pleasure. His eternal song lives in all.

Man and woman are His sweetest tune of the heavenly waves. You can try to measure the distance between middle C and a gazillionth note higher, or you can pause and just listen to God's beautiful tunes. When you listen, put away all your expectations and just listen to the song of life!

We are so concerned with what everything means that we miss the beauty everything wants to show us about the one who made it all. There are things of God's handiwork that sing a song reserved for only the willing and obedient. "He makes me to lie down in green pastures. He leads me beside the still waters. He restores my soul" (Psalm 23:2-3). What does that sound like? Have you ever stopped for a moment in a verdant valley and just soaked in the fullness of it all? What does a vibrant, thriving valley sound like? You can appreciate the songs of its season only by just being there. But I can help you out just a bit.

Under the winter snows His awesome beauty cuddles beneath as the sun shines soft and comfy. The life underneath thrives in it's waiting to stretch and yawn and sing. And when rest is done, the blanket of white gives the food that creation needs to prosper in the seasons changes.

The song of spring sings of sunlight gently striking the brilliant crystal shell as drips and drops play on invisible strings on the air and sky and breath. The currents flow with melted snows as they push through to the other side of the old song that is new once again.

A new path has been made for the life that awakens from the momentary sleep to thrive and sing in the water courses that play and dance through the land. The inhabitants move about and prosper, the valley folk greet each other one more time and waltz to the tunes of love's soft wooing.

The grass leaps up. The trees stretch their limbs and drink the sun. The crawling, creeping, leaping, and running things repeat the eternal tune of thanksgiving to God, "I am here!" We come to see what manner of life is there and hear the voice of nature. And if we are truly there, we will hear our Father in heaven echo the valley's greeting: "I AM here! I have always been here waiting for you to come back to Me and rest.".

The birds sing, "Come and see.". The soft breezes plead softly, "Come and stay for a while. He is here.". Our heavenly Father speaks to us in every blade, blossom, gently swaying branch, every hum and buzz and click and call. The message to all is "I AM here.".

In our minds, the distance between two points takes our focus forward, but if we take time to listen to the heart of love, it's everything in between that makes the trip worth taking. Ask a mountain climber, "Why do you climb this mountain?", and expect the answer. "Because it's there.". That lack of logic used to worry me. I had a terrible fear of heights. But what does the mountain say to the man or woman who dares try its cracks and crevices? "I AM here.". Everywhere we go, in every nook and cranny, every height and depth, every plain and valley, God calls, "I AM here, I AM here.". He waits in the season's comings and goings for us to answer Him. When we hear all His creation, we are preparing our hearts to hear of His love, to hear His voice of love.

To every man and woman, there is a lifetime of listening. What we hear is our perception of life; we create pictures in our minds of it. What we hear and choose to accept helps preserve us or prevent us while we are here. But because of the fall of the man and the woman, our ears are dulled from hearing the good stuff; what our minds expect to see is an uncaring, wrathful Father who is angry with us.

It bears repeating until we get it in our minds that God loved us before anything was something. That something became us. He never gave up on us, and He calls to us through His beloved Son Jesus. Hear His words of loving and care:

"O Lord, You have searched me and known me.

You know my sitting down and my rising up; You understand my thought afar off. You comprehend my path and my lying down,

And are acquainted with all my ways. For there is not a word on my tongue,

But behold, O Lord, You know it altogether.

You have hedged me behind and before, And laid Your hand upon me.

Such knowledge is too wonderful for me;

It is high, I cannot attain it.

Where can I go from Your Spirit?

Or where can I flee from Your presence?

If I ascend into heaven, You are there;

If I make my bed in hell, behold, You are there. If I take the wings of the morning,

And dwell in the uttermost parts of the sea,

Even there Your hand shall lead me,

And Your right hand shall hold me. If I say, "Surely the darkness shall fall on me,"

Even the night shall be light about me;

Indeed, the darkness shall not hide from You,

But the night shines as the day;

The darkness and the light are both alike to You.

For You formed my inward parts;

You covered me in my mother's womb.

I will praise You, for I am fearfully and wonderfully made;

Marvelous are Your works,

And that my soul knows very well.

My frame was not hidden from You,

When I was made in secret,

And skillfully wrought in the lowest parts of the earth.

Your eyes saw my substance, being yet unformed.

And in Your book they all were written,
The days fashioned for me,
When as yet there were none of them.
How precious also are Your thoughts to me, O God!
How great is the sum of them!
If I should count them, they would be more in number than the sand;
When I awake, I am still with You.
Oh, that You would slay the wicked, O God!
Depart from me, therefore, you bloodthirsty men.
For they speak against You wickedly;
Your enemies take Your name in vain.
Do I not hate them, O Lord, who hate You?
And do I not loathe those who rise up against You?
I hate them with perfect hatred;
I count them my enemies. Search me,
O God, and know my heart;
Try me, and know my anxieties;
And see if there is any wicked way in me,
And lead me in the way everlasting." (Psalm 139: 1-24).

The life as a man and as a woman is the song we sing whether in darkness or in the Light. We will hear and sing what is in our hearts. But that is not the end of it.

Though the season's cycles sing the same song, it is never exactly the same. Each time, the song becomes more beautiful and draws all the nearer to the Creator. The passion and longing swells like a river breaking its banks. Life will flow and expand and won't stop until every space between the notes are filled with God's voice singing, "I AM here, I AM here!".

His Words are His instructions to us, but we have a hard time believing it could be that simple. Faith is simple; all we have to do is believe. It's like listening to a favorite song. You focus on it. You remember what it means to you, and when the comfort of that memory takes over, you dance in aisles of the grocery store or 'lose yourself in the moments while driving. Music does something to us; God made us that way to help us get back to Him.

The next time you go to the park or playground, listen the sounds of life. The laughter. The dance of drips and drops of vibrant life exploding all around. Then listen closer and hear love songs singing to you. Each person. Each passing car. Each gust of wind. Every click, pop, snap, crack, buzz, hum and whisper are all singing the note of God's awesome miracle of love so you can hear Him say, "I AM here, I Am here!"

Every man and woman walks the path of life in a rush to get past its hard or painful elements. We miss each other because of our hurry. We are God's songs to each other. The dance of life isn't a solo but a ballet danced by whoever comes our way.

God our Creator made us to find the allegro and dolci of His heart to walk hand in hand with Him, and so with the man and the woman. When we strive with The Gracious One we bring destruction to the beautiful chorus whose purpose is to get to us to lie down in green pastures and listen. To walk beside the still water. To be restored in our souls. Because of our clouded vision, we have to put aside much before we can see what's really there. We must decide to stop and listen. When we walk and talk in fear for sin and shame, death and darkness, our ears are filled with the many voices that only tear us down. In this path, we feel separated when we strain to hear His love song, "I AM here.". But if we stop and ask as dear children we will find the quiet place reserved just for us, where we can find who we are in Him, who we are to each other, and where He is leading us to.

When you close your eyes and ponder all that is streaming into your ear gate, you see what manner of God He is. You see Him in the song, and you dance with Him in the dance of life. You remember who brought you here.

Our association with life is grounded in our past conversations and bits of passing words that taught us how to communicate with each other. In our learning, we have adapted with the disability of prejudgment of the people in our day. The imagery is comedic and satirical because we have decided certain people will speak certain way.

Just to find out how wrong you can be, try going to a place you have passed by but never took the time to be a part of. Sit, close your eyes, and imagine who the people walking by look like.

Then open your eyes. You'll probably laugh at the discrepancy between imagination and reality, but don't laugh too loud; they might consider you rude.

When I worked at Kbyte in Gaylord, Michigan, I worked with a very colorful crowd. It was there that I met my now deceased wife Lori.

An older man would make announcements over the intercom. Lori was sure that he was very masculine and attractive in person, based solely on his voice. The guy looked like Elmer Fudd, the original one before bugs bunny came in technicolor. The man was short and fat. He had the same face of Elmer Fudd, right down to the long eye lashes and big floppy ears. It was all in his voice that she heard and what she imagined him to be like.

Did you ever imagine how someone you're talking to on the phone looks? Blue Sky Animation has produced four Ice Age animated productions. In Ice Age—The Continental Drift is a pirate character named Gut, a large, blue, funky-looking ape. His voice fills the room when he speaks. In the recording studio, a man barely three feet tall, spoke Gut's lines in the voice over.

Did you ever listen to others without looking to see how old they were? Again and again, we err humorously because we don't really know what we know. We try to see how pretty, distinguished, intelligent, successful, or weak people are by their voices.

We project our memories of people with similar voices onto those we listen to, and then we laugh when we meet the new people and see how wrong we were. Life can be hilarious; those we meet can become colorful additions to our treasured memories. Consider the strong, silent type males, the ones with bulging muscles but closed mouths. They are silent for a reason. If you ever hear them speak your laughter would get you into a bit of trouble with them. God's sense of humor. He wants us to keep from taking life too seriously. After all He is the God of joy.

It is His creation. His world. He does what pleases Him. he paints a picture for us in this Psalm.

> "Praise the Lord!
> Praise the Lord from the heavens;
> Praise Him in the heights!
> Praise Him, all His angels; Praise Him, all His hosts!
> Praise Him, sun and moon;
> Praise Him, all you stars of light!
> Praise Him, you heavens of heavens, And you waters above the heavens!
> Let them praise the name of the Lord,
> For He commanded and they were created.
> He also established them forever and ever;
> He made a decree which shall not pass away.
> Praise the Lord from the earth,
> You great sea creatures and all the depths;
> Fire and hail, snow and clouds;
> Stormy wind, fulfilling His word;
> Mountains and all hills;
> Fruitful trees and all cedars;
> Beasts and all cattle;
> Creeping things and flying fowl;
> Kings of the earth and all peoples;
> Princes and all judges of the earth;
> Both young men and maidens;
> Old men and children.
> Let them praise the name of the Lord,
> For His name alone is exalted;
> His glory is above the earth and heaven.
> And He has exalted the horn of His people,
> The praise of all
> His saints— Of the children of Israel,
> A people near to Him.
> Praise the Lord! (Psalm 148: 1-14)

CHAPTER 6

We Are All Broken

We live in a culture that defines people, places, and things much the way that animal, vegetable, and mineral apply to the reality we have presumed to be. We separate people by social, ethnic or ideological classification that have nothing to do with reason or rhyme.

All we have accepted as truth is so much less than what God's Word says it is. Because of the barriers of religious prejudice and stereotyping, we don't see each other's needs in the same way our heavenly Father does.

I literally put on a lot of miles to find myself. My quest was to find out if love was really out there. Along the way, I felt the chill of extreme emptiness. My heart felt a hurt that went beyond any words. Psalm 102 is dead on.

"For my days are consumed like smoke, And my bones are burned like a hearth.

My heart is stricken and withered like grass, So that I forget to eat my bread.

Because of the sound of my groaning My bones cling to my skin.

I am like a pelican of the wilderness; I am like an owl of the desert. I lie awake, And am like a sparrow alone on the housetop." (Psalm 102:3-7).

I didn't come from a loving family. My broken heart led me down reckless paths. I hitchhiked a lot in my youth searching for something undefinable. One night in Levering, Michigan, I felt the chill of the night air and an aloneness that made me shudder. In the midnight hour, I listened to roaring semis in the distance reminding me of where I was. There was no other traffic. In the waiting for a ride I just turned south and started walking to the next town.

A hunter's moon kept me company. There was not a passing car or truck. Not a single animal passed me by. I heard in the quiet of the morning and the sound of my feet as I plodded. With the bright moon on my shoulder, I walked into the hour of the rising sun. I had walked thirteen miles. A gunsmith who met me on his way through stopped his truck and gave me a ride. He was most hospitable to serve me breakfast. A gift of God's mercy. As I think on it.

We all search for God in our own way. But in the end of our search, it is the same for us all—a simple turn to see who is watching over us, who has never left our side and won't well into eternity.

In my brokenness, I walked many miles searching many faces to see if love was there. It was. But I was still blinded by my expectation of what I thought I would see and hear. What did love look like? It took me a long time to discover that love wasn't out there, it was nearby, and that we're all looking for the same thing.

It just took a few trips around the same desert to understand I didn't need to climb the highest mountain to find that something for my empty heart. I found that all I needed to do was turn around to see the One who loved us much that He willingly died on the cross beaten and bloody for me and you all. I concluded I was searching for completion of my heart and a place I could call home. My destination was God's heart and the hearts of those who love Him. My heavenly Father has always loved me just as it is in heaven. I found that all I needed to do was to turn and look up to see my Savior who has always waited for me to come back home. I am family.

We are all lost without love and for someone to love us right where we are. We are all broken in the same way. We all walk this path of loneliness but cannot see each other because darkness covers our eyes. When the light of love and truth comes into our hearts, we can see that love was going ahead of us to prepare a way and was behind us to watch our backs. That's when we can see each other. We just need to reach out in faith into this darkened vale and believe that someone on the other side will be there to pull us through.

When the Light of the World stepped into my darkness, I saw the rest of the world in the same shape I was in—lost without hope apart from Him. Walking in the light of His love, I began seeing things we all miss, mostly each other. We need each other to get on in this life because that is how God made it to be.

Turn with me into the glory of heaven come to earth, the love of our heavenly Father incarnate Jesus. Let us follow Him into eternity. We need to know many important things to get back to fellowship with our Father, to walk and talk with Him and see His beautiful face of love. God's Word has clearly revealed the path we ought to take. I invite you to read on with me and let us see together how great a love our heavenly Father lavished upon us (Romans 8: 37-39).

Our understanding begins with knowing the state of our soul as we surrender to Him, making Him the center of our life. Hear the words of Jesus our Savior:

"I am the true vine, and My Father is the vinedresser. Every branch in Me that does not bear fruit He takes away; and every branch that bears fruit He prunes, that it may bear more fruit. You are already clean because of the word which I have spoken to you. Abide in Me, and I in you. As the branch cannot bear fruit of itself, unless it abides in the vine, neither can you, unless you abide in Me.

I am the vine, you are the branches. He who abides in Me, and I in him, bears much fruit; for without Me you can do nothing. If anyone does not abide in Me, he is cast out as a branch and is withered; and they gather them and throw them into the fire, and they are burned. If you abide in Me, and My words abide in you, you will ask what you desire, and it shall be done for you. By this My Father is glorified, that you bear much fruit; so you will be My disciples." (John 15:1-8).

The first steps of faith are the same for all who come. All have sinned and have fallen short of the glory of God (Romans 3:23). There is no one who is righteous (Romans 3: 10). We can do nothing without Jesus. We are nothing without Jesus. For in Him and through Him all things live and breathe. He is the Door through which we enter into fellowship with our heavenly Father (John 10:7). The gift of salvation it is His gift of grace. No one can earn it or receive it through lineage (Ephesians 2:1-10). How then we might be saved? Through repentance and the shed blood of Jesus on the cross the spotless Lamb of God (John 1:29).

We need our heavenly Father to show us the way back home. We should just turn, look into His wonderful face, and follow His voice. We are the sheep of His pasture, and no other voice can we follow in life to prepare us for the life to come (John 10: I 1-16). God being God, you can expect from Him the perfect five step and the ten step plan, one step and another and another and another, until we cross the finish line, our final breath, which will usher us into living again and again for always.

I say it again. The walk of faith is simple. He leads you, you follow. And when you do not understand ask Him. He will tell you. In faith you walk and talk with Him where He is, in heavenly places. He is here with you right now, right where you are, right now.

Love is God's plan for a perfect life. Love the Lord your God with all your heart, with all your mind, and with all your strength. And love your neighbor as yourself. On these two commandments hang all the law and the prophets (Leviticus 19: 18; Deuteronomy 6:5; John 14:15).

In our brokenness, we stand before all creation. We walk this earth for a brief season. We are called by the power of the Holy Spirit of Jesus, to be sons and daughters of the Living God with complete access to our heavenly Father through Jesus Christ (Ephesians 4:1-6; I Peter 2:940). We are in this world but not of this world (John 8:23). Herein lies the battle for all of us, society has a caste system that tries to limit the full power of the church from functioning as a living people of God. We have the truth of the gospel, His written word telling the story of the Living Word Jesus the Christ, the Messiah Come. It is our religious culture that hinders our knowing and living in the fullness of his plan. His law is living in the liberty of holiness led by His Holy Spirit. Tradition and legalism will never ever replace the relationship we are meant to have with our heavenly Father. The old law was to bring us to the Door, Jesus The Way. He has come and the law of sin is dead in us through His shed blood and the cross for us to receive from His heart God's Son for all who may come (Psalm 36:8; John 1:16; Romans 11:25; Galatians 4:4; Ephesians 1:10, 3:19; Colossians 2:9). The law of love is liberty. We have been set free. Our chains are gone (1 Corinthians 3:16-18; Luke 4:18; Romans 8:21; 2 Corinthians 3:17; James 1:25).

The foolish stumble over the sacraments, baptism in water, baptism of the Holy Spirit; forgetting that it is God who gives and dispenses the gifts of salvation and manifests His Holy Spirit in us, through us, and around us. The basic truth of our salvation is our being covered by the shed blood of The Holy Lamb of God, Jesus the Christ and being welcomed into the fellowship with our Father in heaven through Jesus, His Holy Spirit comes to live in us. It is God who takes way the sins of the world. It is God who shall avenge all wrong doing on earth. It is God our Father in heaven who gives and takes away. We who believe and follow Jesus our Savior are of one spirit, His Holy Spirit. The gift of tongues, prophecy, healings, discernment, etc. and whatever equips the church to do the work of God, which is to believe in the one whom God sent, are not ours to determine. We are called to submit ourselves one to another in respect to God's calling as sons and daughters of God. His Holy Spirit will reprove and correct. Our job is to do what Jesus said to do. Love God and love one another, the power to live and live again are through Him alone and anyone who says different or tries to lead us away from this truth is a liar and an antichrist. The evidence that we are His children is by our love to each other and for each other, as we reach back to the lost, hurting and broken; to tell of His grace, to share His peace and rest. Jesus is The Way, The Great Shepherd. We are His completely or not at all, If we are His He will profess us as His own before His Father in heaven. If we are not, He will deny us before His Father in heaven (Matthew 10:33 & 16:24).

When we profess to be Christians, believers in Jesus the Messiah; The Christ, The way; we proclaim to the world, the powers of darkness, to all dominions; that we serve the Lord Jesus, who is King and Lord of all of heaven and earth for always. We give ourselves over completely in service to Him and Him alone. No other will we follow. He has given us the power to be His children, His sons and daughters, as we surrender to Him in love, (Matthew 6:24, Galatians 5:13).

God is the God of yesterday, today and tomorrow. He is forever and ever. There is no shadow of turning with Him (James 1: 16-18; Psalm 29: 10; 45:6, 146:10). As His people, we have no right to say who shall enter into His loving arms and eternal fellowship. God does the telling; we who are His follow Him. We are accountable to rightly divide the word of truth and to discern the faithful from the false. We have the Holy Spirit of Jesus, who is one with God. He dwells in us and makes us one body. We will know each other by our love for each other (John 10:30; I Corinthians 12: 14; Galatians 5: 13; Ephesians 4:4-6). This is the power of God in us that we love God and serve Him by loving each other, serving one another as unto Him.

We are all the least of these (Mark 9:37). He is all we need. He is our All in All, our Great Provider, Healer, King, Lord, Friend, Eternal Father, Lamb of God, and Light of the World. To say that God will let loose His power on earth in us in the measure we feel comfortable with is grounds for a butt whipping. The law of His liberty is to walk in the fullness of His power in His presence now and forever, to move and breathe in the beauty of His holiness.

We mark the times of revival by the people God raised up, but what God did for the people at the time is too easily forgotten. The remembrance is lost when the people who were the living tale and the cause for which they were raised are forgotten. When we fail to give God the glory for what He has done, we become blinded to His merciful hand that lifts us.

In our present generation, we have a people who have followed a church culture but have not heard the truth. The vision of the people is polluted by ungrateful hearts full of themselves. We have a method of evangelism, but the evangelist is absent. We keep names and lift them as a banner that does not glorify God, and we use it to keep the truth from being preached to the lost world. The lost need to see Jesus as He is—an almighty, risen Savior, King, and Lord of All who reigns forever.

The young see the half-truth the religious culture has presented, they long to see the invincible, eternal Son of God who sits at the right hand of God in heaven. Our society lives in fear for the lack of love. The need for answers can only be resolved with a face to face. With Jesus in us. Our face. We are His hands and feet. The lost need to hear from you.

The walking oracles of His love, those of us who profess Him as our Lord and Savior, are called to speak the words He wants them to hear. His breath is living in us. His light of truth saves that which was lost. I say again, we who believe are His hands and feet. He commands us to reach out to take the hand of the lost and broken, the one nearest you with the greatest need, to tell His story of love with our lives, our deeds, and our words, of His amazing grace.

We cannot maintain to be His and remain divided over matters that are not ours to judge. We who are called are His. It is His truth All things live in Him. All things having been created by Him, will return to Him. God is God. We are not.

Just as we would be cited for an infraction or honored for a good deed, so it is with our heavenly Father. All that we do is noted to honor or dishonor. And all accounts will be settled. Be sure of it by the one who gives and takes away. All we do and say is seen and heard by all heaven, the principalities and powers of darkness and all creation. What we do matters to all the spirit world and all creation. Every creature and all the earth groan in longing for the sons and daughters of God to rise up and take their place of authority once again. Decide well and you shall do well. Decide poorly and you will fall away and be cast into outer darkness.

We are to be the sons and daughters of the Living God. We have the Word of God to show us His plan of redemption. We have His Son, Jesus, to follow. We have the Holy Spirit of Jesus, who empowers us to be the sons and daughters of God. We have each other to work with, love, and serve with and for. We have the lost world that wants to be found and set free of sin, shame, fear, death, and darkness whether it knows it or not.

When you let Jesus into your heart, the God of the universe comes to live in you. He loves, keeps, and saves you. He is with you eternally. Take a step of faith and see how much He loves you. Reach out and see how much he loves the people to whom you are sent. Take that step of faith to love the one nearest you and begin together to walk in the power of His love.

As we lift the fallen, take the hand of the fallen and let us rise as a continuous wave of spiritual renewal and stand in the glory of His awesome love. No one will ever be turned away; all who come are welcome. Come as you are, and walk in accordance with the passage of God's everlasting promise:

"Finally, my brethren, be strong in the Lord and in the power of His might. Put on the whole armor of God, that you may be able to stand against the wiles of the devil. For we do not wrestle against flesh and blood, but against principalities, against powers, against the rulers of the darkness of this age, against spiritual hosts of wickedness in the heavenly places. Therefore take up the whole armor of God, that you may be able to withstand in the evil day, and having done all, to stand.

Stand therefore, having girded your waist with truth, having put on the breastplate of righteousness, and having shod your feet with the preparation of the gospel of peace; above all, taking the shield of faith with which you will be able to quench all the fiery darts of the wicked one. And take the helmet of salvation, and the sword of the Spirit, which is the word of God; praying always with all prayer and supplication in the Spirit, being watchful to this end with all perseverance and supplication for all the saints— and for me, that utterance may be given to me, that I may open my mouth boldly to make known the mystery of the gospel, for which I am an ambassador in chains; that in it I may speak boldly, as I ought to speak." (Ephesians 6: 10-20).

Stay standing in the power of His awesome love and unending mercy and grace.

CHAPTER 7

The Voice We Know

The faithless, well-educated people, the men and woman who say that there is a thousand percent of something have tried to convince society that our embryonic development and our early childhood memories will ever remain vague to us. But God our Creator, in His mercy reveals our life to us from our very beginning; in His seasons of dispensations. We remember what we went through. God leads us back to Him through the wonder of our record of events. It is hard to say what we shall recall at His beconning. They are special moments showing us that He was always there keeping us, singing His love song over us. In truth I say such knowledge is so profound the words bear repeating again and again.

My childhood wasn't much of one. My father abandoned my mother, siblings, and me several times until I was about seven. That's when he left for good to Nebraska with another man's wife and her children. I don't have good memories of my father. But as God was revealing Himself to me I have memories that are unspeakable and quite wonderful. My heavenly Father was always there even before I was a twinkle in my parent's eyes. Such knowledge is so profound it is worth repeating until we understand how much our Father in heaven loves us. Hear His words of love and caring again:

"For You formed my inward parts;
You covered me in my mother's womb.
I will praise You, for I am fearfully and wonderfully made;
Marvelous are Your works,
And that my soul knows very well.
My frame was not hidden from You,
When I was made in secret,
And skillfully wrought in the lowest parts of the earth.
Your eyes saw my substance, being yet unformed.
And in Your book they all were written,
The days fashioned for me,
When as yet there were none of them.
How precious also are Your thoughts to me, O God!
How great is the sum of them!
If I should count them, they would be more in number than the sand;
When I awake, I am still with You.". (Psalm 139:13-18)

Our Lord God started the conversation long before I could utter a word, but somehow, I heard Him and knew Him as my heavenly Father. On my way back to Him, I am learning His blessings for me to hear Him and see Him just as He is before all creation.

As I take my steps of faith, I remember what my Father said and when He said it. This chapter is the revelation that came to me well into my latter years, after all my falling and rising and returning to His side to face Him and walk with Him. This overview is what the Holy Spirit of Jesus has reopened to me to let me see where I was and where I am going.

THE VOICE

When I was just conceived, I didn't have ears to hear or eyes to see. I wasn't much to look at. But I knew that I was. I was someone. I could feel my heart beating and saying, "Live!

After a while, I heard my heart say, "Grow!". And soon, I had fingers and toes, a cute little nose, and eyes to see and ears to hear.

In time, my comfortable space became cramped. I was afraid. My heart said, "Out!".

I was angry and confused in my cold, busy new place. But I heard a soft voice. My mother's voice. The word she spoke was, "Love.", but I became worried because it was not the voice that had first spoken to me when I was but a beating pulse of life. Why has that voice stopped talking to me? I wondered. I wanted to hear that voice. I needed to hear that voice. I listened to every voice hoping it was that voice again. Time passed. That gentle calm voice I longed to hear would not speak to me.

Anger, fear and confusion overcame me. I wanted to run away, but my little feet didn't know how to do that. I could barely lift my head. In my rage, I made quite a fuss. I wanted to make sure someone heard me.

So lived and grew. All the while, something was missing. Someone was missing. I had to find who and what it was. The voice was still silent. "Where are you?", I asked. "I've listened for your voice. I hoped you would say something. Anything! Let me know you're there.".

But all I heard was silence. My anger and fear and confusion consumed me. I could not go far, but I began to search for that voice. I could only cry, hoping someone would carry me in my search. I cried "Help me! Wherever I go, I look for you. I want to hear you!".

I grew. I learned to walk without stumbling. I searched for that voice. One day, I saw something I wanted. I couldn't reach it, so I cried out in anger. My mother said, "Ask.". I did. She gave —me what I wanted. Everyone gave me what I wanted. But I didn't get what I needed—that small, calm voice.

There were times I asked for things that were not safe for me to have, things that were not good for me. I was very angry and afraid. I did everything I was told to do. "Why can't I have what I asked for?". My mother said a strange word. "No". I became more angry and more afraid and even more confused. I lived. I grew. I asked. I obeyed. I did everything I was told to do. "Why can't I have what I want if I do what I was told to do? Why can't you hear me?".

One day, my mother took my hand and led me to a strange place. Other mothers and children were there standing in a line. My mother told me, "Wait.".

"Why?", I asked her.

My mother did not answer.

I decided I would no longer listen. I would find what I wanted on my own and take it. I didn't know what that missing something was, only that I would find it somehow, some way. I searched in the only way I knew how—in fear, anger, and confusion. On my journey, I heard many voices. Something felt wrong inside me. I did not live. I did not grow. I did not ask. I did not wait. I did not love. I died inside.

I heard so many voices speaking that I just quit listening to all of them. I stopped listening to everything. I couldn't hear that small, calm voice that had first spoken to me. I was lost. I was afraid. I was alone. I was empty.

I decided to fill the emptiness with things that I would take. At first, I took little things so no one would notice they were missing. But in time, I took bigger and bigger things. I quit listening and people quit hearing me. I didn't trust. I continued to die inside. Part of me cried out to hear that small, calm voice, but heavy things like murder and hate smothered it. And the voice that screamed for help was silent. Or so I thought.

I convinced myself I couldn't find that missing something. I didn't need anyone. I did what I was told to do, but I didn't get what I wanted. I felt the horrible chill of utter loneliness.

I screamed, "Is anybody out there? Is anybody listening to me? Does anybody see me?".

I did terrible things in my search to fill the emptiness, but the emptiness just grew. The anger grew. I was so afraid that I could only stumble in my confusion.

Then one day, I raised my hand to do great harm. A voice I faintly remember said, "Stop!". The chill that filled my mind, body, and soul was so overwhelming that I couldn't move. I had to listen. That's all I could do. I tried to find out where the voice was coming from. I couldn't see the person speaking. But the voice was beside me.

I wanted to run away. In my anger and fear, I took a step but stumbled and fell to my knees. The weight of my emptiness was so heavy that I bowed under it. Every joint in my body screamed in pain. I was being crushed and broken. I discovered it wasn't my body that was being torn apart; it was my heart. I tried to resist in the pain in my anger and fear, but I couldn't rise by my own strength.

The voice spoke again. "Pray.".

"I don't understand. I don't pray. I don't know how to pray.".

The voice said, "Jesus.".

The ache in my heart hurt so badly that I could barely breathe. Somehow, I exhaled, "Jesus!".

The voice that had been beside me started speaking from my heart. The voice said, "Forgiveness!".

The chill of loneliness left me. For the first time I could remember I felt warm and safe. I was embraced by a presence I knew long ago. As I bowed the small, calm voice that spoke to me long before I was said, "Walk.".

The weight of all my anger, fear, and confusion lifted. I felt His hand take mine and help me to my feet. I smiled and wept as I heard the words I had longed for. From within my heart, He said, "Live again.".

As I reexamine my life after Lori's going home on November 30, 2013, I draw closer to my Father and rediscover the person I had put aside for many years. These words of rediscovery make much more sense to me now; I see the full picture the bits and pieces of my life have come to be. The person God wanted me to become is looking up more and more. I better understand where I have been, why I was there, and what really happened.

The power to live and love grows in me every day; the pain, anger, and fear are healed in my heart. I have always been who I was; it just took me all this time to see the man I am in God's reflection. I see His good in me. I see all the time He invested in me. I rest in His care and reflect on the quiet hours when the weight of this life was so great that all I could do was stand still and breathe and wait on Him. Jesus waited for me my whole life just to tell me how much He has always loved me.

We don't know just how much He loves us until we see His proven love through our days coming and going, rising up and going out, and coming in and lying down. It is so great a love that we cannot fully comprehend its dimensions. His love has always been there for us before even time began.

Before Jesus was arrested and willingly went to the cross for us, He prayed in the garden of Gethsemane. To understand how Jesus felt for us before anything was at all. We need to know what He said in those difficult hours. The disciple, His familial brother, son of Joseph; gave us His words, as John was there in person and by His Holy Spirit wrote them down for posterity. They read thusly:

"Father, the hour has come. Glorify Your Son, that Your Son also may glorify You, as You have given Him authority over all flesh, that He should give eternal life to as many as You have given Him. And this is eternal life, that they may know You, the only true God, and Jesus Christ whom You have sent. I have glorified You on the earth. I have finished the work which You have given Me to do. And now, O Father, glorify Me together with Yourself, with the glory which I had with You before the world was.

I have manifested Your name to the men whom You have given Me out of the world. They were Yours, You gave them to Me, and they have kept Your word. Now they have known that all things which You have given Me are from You. For I have given to them the words which You have given Me; and they have received them, and have known surely that I came forth from You; and they have believed that You sent Me.

I pray for them. I do not pray for the world but for those whom You have given Me, for they are Yours. And all Mine are Yours, and Yours are Mine, and I am glorified in them. Now I am no longer in the world, but these are in the world, and I come to You. Holy Father, keep through Your name those whom You have given Me, that they may be one as We are. While I was with them in the world, I kept them in Your name. Those whom You gave Me I have kept; and none of them is lost except the son of perdition, that the Scripture might be fulfilled. But now I come to You, and these things I speak in the world, that they may have My joy fulfilled in themselves. I have given them Your word; and the world has hated them because they are not of the world, just as I am not of the world. I do not pray that You should take them out of the world, but that You should keep them from the evil one. They are not of the world, just as I am not of the world. Sanctify them by Your truth. Your word is truth. As You sent Me into the world, I also have sent them into the world, And for their sakes I sanctify Myself, that they also may be sanctified by the truth.

I do not pray for these alone, but also for those who will believe in Me through their word; that they all may be one, as You, Father, are in Me, and I in You; that they also may be one in Us, that the world may believe that You sent Me. And the glory which You gave Me I have given them, that they may be one just as We are one: I in them, and You in Me; that they may be made perfect in one, and that the world may know that You have sent Me, and have loved them as You have loved Me.

Father, I desire that they also whom You gave Me may be with Me where I am, that they may behold My glory which You have given Me; for You loved Me before the foundation of the world. O righteous Father! The world has not known You, but I have known You; and these have known that You sent Me. And I have declared to them Your name, and will declare it, that the love with which You loved Me may be in them, and I in them." (John 17: 1-26 NKJV).

Jesus saw me and the life I would live and still came to me and is with me, a person who was not a person of a people who were not as yet a people but are now through faith.

Our Father in heaven will meet us every step of the way through our lives. Whether rising or falling, winning, or losing, He has promised to keep us; all we need to do is lift up our eyes to see His lovely face, take His hand, and walk with Him.

Our gentle Shepherd calls you. How will you answer?

CHAPTER 8

The Life You Keep

Life began with a promise from the only true promise keeper, our heavenly Father. God cannot lie; He is truth (John 14:6, 16:13, 17:17).

We can hear the truth, but we do not always follow it. Sometimes, our next step is in the opposite direction because we need just a bit more convincing to give up doing things our way. More often than not, that's the nature of our hearts. We even have a kind of stone named after our sinful nature, adamantine, one of the hardest rocks on earth. It fits us perfectly.

Everything about us apart from the Lord God is contrary and quite independent of reason or rhyme. We just are or we are not---there's no middle ground between good and bad. But what's worse is knowing the truth and walking away from it. Hence, the Lord's warning, "Do not harden your hearts as the children of Israel did in the wilderness" (Psalm 95:8-1 1). Out of the original million or so people that were in the exodus out of the land of Egypt only a few made it to see the promised land: Joshua and all his house and Caleb and all his house. God blessed them for their obedience to be a continuation of the legacy promise that God, I AM made to Abraham. (Numbers 27:18-23; 13:16-25, 14:6-9, and 27, 30:5-9, 24-38).

It is our advantage to work through the bad stuff and keep the good stuff at the ending of the moment of hardship. That's the best plan of action to come out of any situation a winner. By God's standard, it is the measure of forgiveness with which we live in Him wherein we find the benefits of His rest for the time being and the treasure of eternal rest later.

But there is a catch to letting go and letting God take over your life; you have to let go of what's in your hands to hold onto what HE has prepared for you now and not too much later. The later will be here very shortly in the blink of an eye. Get ready.

What we keep in this life is like our breath and blood. Whom we serve in this life is the evidence of what we have to look forward to as we look into the mirror every morning.

"What does it profit us to gain the world but lose our souls?" (Matthew 10:28, 16:26). We can gain everything and lose everything in a heartbeat. It's good to first listen and then act (James 1: 19). The things worth keeping are clearly definable. We can see them throughout all our days. Whatever is of good and is good is from God (James 1: 17). We are to meditate on whatever is true, noble, just, pure, lovely, of good report, or praiseworthy (Philippians 4:8-9).

These helpful hints will aid us in staying focused, but bear in mind that it is always a walk of faith from breath to breath and step by step. The beginning of wisdom is fear of the Lord (Job 28: 28; Psalm I 11:10, Proverbs 9:10). To fear God is not to shudder in His presence but to understand your relationship with Him.

His joy is our strength. His good pleasure in our lives is the heart's desire of every man and woman born again.

All creation waits for us to walk with our Father in heaven. We live in the end times awaiting His return, but we cannot know why we wait and whom we wait for until we know the One who is coming back to gather the church, the body of Christ. Learning of Him is the first step we take toward Him when we rise to see every new day. So many people have come and gone; their memory is all too often buried with their passing. But some memories mark the times and place and remind us that someone was here with something to say.

We were created by the Lord God in His image. We are His handiwork. All things were made by Him, for Him, for we are His good pleasure. We live unto Him. We die unto Him. And during the days between the spark of life and our last breath, we learn of Him and each other. The stories we tell live in the air, the trees, the rocks, and the paths we take. With every sunrise and sunset, we hear the legend and see the song that sings in the people of the land and see Him.

Since my wife went home after a life of diabetes, I began my journey back to myself. Our final place of end of life caring was on Aloha Drive in Alanson, Michigan. As a husband, I learned much about the loving and living and losing that come with life. We never know what we will give until we are presented with the greatest need of the one we dearly love.

After Jesus rose from the grave, He let the world know He was among us. There is evidence through legend and lore of a being as bright as the sun that came to every tribe, clan, and people on earth, Jesus went everywhere to show Himself to His creation. The Algonquin of the Little Traverse Bay area remembered and I remembered with them, that as the sun has risen, the Son has risen in us.

Across the Atlantic, another seafaring people heard of the news of Jesus, the Son of God come to us; the people of Colosse. For them, the telling of Jesus came in the act of loving by an apostle named Paul. The record of Paul's words to the people of Colosse are in a letter aptly titled Colossians. On Paul's journey to share the words of Jesus with the people of Ephesus, he came upon a sleepy little town called Colosse. It was once a thriving merchant town, a center of commerce for the coastal region it serviced. The people were already a devoted community accustomed to worship and religious devotion. The one thing they lacked was the truth of God the Father in heaven and the Son of God come to save them all. They needed to hear the message of the redemption and surrender to the Living God. In His letter, Paul told them of all God had in store for those who surrendered to Him and of what God required of them to follow. The words of our beloved brother Paul the apostle to the people of Collosse and to all who may come and believe:

Paul, an apostle of Jesus Christ by the will of God, and Timothy our brother, To the saints and faithful brethren in Christ who are in Colosse: Grace to you and peace from God our Father and the Lord Jesus Christ.

We give thanks to the God and Father of our Lord Jesus Christ, praying always for you, since we heard of your faith in Christ Jesus and of your love for all the saints; because of the hope which is laid up for you in heaven, of which you heard before in the word of the truth of the gospel, which has come to you, as it has also in all the world, and is bringing forth fruit, as it is also among you since the day you heard and knew the grace of God in truth; as you also learned from Epaphras, our dear fellow servant, who is a faithful minister of Christ on your behalf, who also declared to us your love in the Spirit.

For this reason we also, since the day we heard it, do not cease to pray for you, and to ask that you may be filled with the knowledge of His will in all wisdom and spiritual understanding; that you may walk worthy of the Lord, fully pleasing Him, being fruitful in every good work and increasing in the knowledge of God; strengthened with all might, according to His glorious power, for all patience and longsuffering with joy; giving thanks to the Father who has qualified us to be partakers of the inheritance of the saints in the light. He has delivered us from the power of darkness and conveyed us into the kingdom of the Son of His love, in whom we have redemption through His blood, the forgiveness of sins.

He is the image of the invisible God, the firstborn over all creation. For by Him all things were created that are in heaven and that are on earth, visible and invisible, whether thrones or dominions or principalities or powers. All things were created through Him and for Him. And He is before all things, and in Him all things consist. And He is the head of the body, the church, who is the beginning, the firstborn from the dead, that in all things He may have the preeminence.

For it pleased the Father that in Him all the fullness should dwell, and by Him to reconcile all things to Himself, by Him, whether things on earth or things in heaven, having made peace through the blood of His cross.

And you, who once were alienated and enemies in your mind by wicked works, yet now He has reconciled in the body of His flesh through death, to present you holy, and blameless, and above reproach in His sight if indeed you continue in the faith, grounded and steadfast, and are not moved away from the hope of the gospel which you heard, which was preached to every creature under heaven, of which I, Paul, became a minister.

I now rejoice in my sufferings for you, and fill up in my flesh what is lacking in the afflictions of Christ, for the sake of His body, which is the church, of which I became a minister according to the stewardship from God which was given to me for you, to fulfill the word of God, the mystery which has been hidden from ages and from generations, but now has been revealed to His saints. To them God willed to make known what are the riches of the glory of this mystery among the Gentiles: which is Christ in you, the hope of glory. Him we preach, warning every man and teaching every man in all wisdom, that we may present every man perfect in Christ Jesus. To this end I also labor, striving according to His working which works in me mightily.

For I want you to know what a great conflict I have for you and those in Laodicea, and for as many as have not seen my face in the flesh, that their hearts may be encouraged, being knit together in love, and attaining to all riches of the full assurance of understanding, to the knowledge of the mystery of God, both of the Father and of Christ, in whom are hidden all the treasures of wisdom and knowledge.

Now this I say lest anyone should deceive you with persuasive words. For though I am absent in the flesh, yet I am with you in spirit, rejoicing [c]to see your good order and the steadfastness of your faith in Christ.

As you therefore have received Christ Jesus the Lord, so walk in Him, rooted and built up in Him and established in the faith, as you have been taught, abounding in it with thanksgiving.

Beware lest anyone cheat you through philosophy and empty deceit, according to the tradition of men, according to the basic principles of the world, and not according to Christ. For in Him dwells all the fullness of the Godhead bodily; and you are complete in Him, who is the head of all principality and power.

In Him you were also circumcised with the circumcision made without hands, by putting off the body [h]of the sins of the flesh, by the circumcision of Christ, buried with Him in baptism, in which you also were raised with Him through faith in the working of God, who raised Him from the dead. And you, being dead in your trespasses and the uncircumcision of your flesh, He has made alive together with Him, having forgiven you all trespasses, having wiped out the handwriting of requirements that was against us, which was contrary to us. And He has taken it out of the way, having nailed it to the cross. Having disarmed principalities and powers, He made a public spectacle of them, triumphing over them in it

So let no one judge you in food or in drink, or regarding a festival or a new moon or sabbaths, which are a shadow of things to come, but the substance is of Christ. Let no one cheat you of your reward, taking delight in false humility and worship of angels, intruding into those things which he has not seen, vainly puffed up by his fleshly mind, and not holding fast to the Head, from whom all the body, nourished and knit together by joints and ligaments, grows with the increase that is from God.

Therefore, if you died with Christ from the basic principles of the world, why, as though living in the world, do you subject yourselves to regulations. "Do not touch, do not taste, do not handle," which all concern things which perish with the using—according to the commandments and doctrines of men? These things indeed have an appearance of wisdom in self-imposed religion, false humility, and [n] neglect of the body, but are of no value against the indulgence of the flesh.

If then you were raised with Christ, seek those things which are above, where Christ is, sitting at the right hand of God. Set your mind on things above, not on things on the earth. For you died, and your life is hidden with Christ in God. When Christ who is our life appears, then you also will appear with Him in glory.

Therefore put to death your members which are on the earth: fornication, uncleanness, passion, evil desire, and covetousness, which is idolatry. Because of these things the wrath of God is coming upon the sons of disobedience, in which you yourselves once walked when you lived in them.

But now you yourselves are to put off all these: anger, wrath, malice, blasphemy, filthy language out of your mouth. Do not lie to one another, since you have put off the old man with his deeds, and have put on the new man who is renewed in knowledge according to the image of Him who created him, where there is neither Greek nor Jew, circumcised nor uncircumcised, barbarian, Scythian, slave nor free, but Christ is all and in all.

Therefore, as the elect of God, holy and beloved, put on tender mercies, kindness, humility, meekness, long suffering; bearing with one another, and forgiving one another, if anyone has a complaint against another; even as Christ forgave you, so you also must do. But above all these things put on love, which is the bond of perfection. And let the peace of God rule in your hearts, to which also you were called in one body; and be thankful. Let the word of Christ dwell in you richly in all wisdom, teaching and admonishing one another in psalms and hymns and spiritual songs, singing with grace in your hearts to the Lord. And whatever you do in word or deed, do all in the name of the Lord Jesus, giving thanks to God the Father through Him.

Wives, submit to your own husbands, as is fitting in the Lord.

Husbands, love your wives and do not be bitter toward them. Children, obey your parents in all things, for this is well pleasing to the Lord.

Fathers, do not provoke your children, lest they become discouraged. Bondservants, obey in all things your masters according to the flesh, not with eye service, as men-pleasers, but in sincerity of heart, fearing God. And whatever you do, do it heartily, as to the Lord and not to men, knowing that from the Lord you will receive the reward of the inheritance; for you serve the Lord Christ. But he who does wrong will be repaid for what he has done, and there is no partiality.

Masters, give your bondservants what is just and fair, knowing that you also have a Master in heaven.

Continue earnestly in prayer, being vigilant in it with thanksgiving; meanwhile praying also for us, that God would open to us a door for the word, to speak the mystery of Christ, for which I am also in chains, that I may make it manifest, as I ought to speak.

Walk in wisdom toward those who are outside, redeeming the time. Let your speech always be with grace, seasoned with salt, that you may know how you ought to answer each one.

Tychicus, a beloved brother, faithful minister, and fellow servant in the Lord, will tell you all the news about me. I am sending him to you for this very purpose, that he may know your circumstances and comfort your hearts, with Onesimus, a faithful and beloved brother, who is one of you. They will make known to you all things which are happening here.

Aristarchus my fellow prisoner greets you, with Mark the cousin of Barnabas (about whom you received instructions: if he comes to you, welcome him), and Jesus who is called Justus. These are my only fellow workers for the kingdom of God who are of the circumcision; they have proved to be a comfort to me.

Epaphras, who is one of you, a bondservant of Christ, greets you, always laboring fervently for you in prayers, that you may stand perfect and [c]complete in all the will of God. For I bear him witness that he has a great zeal for you, and those who are in Laodicea, and those in Hierapolis. Luke the beloved physician and Demas greet you. Greet the brethren who are in Laodicea, and Nymphas and the church that is in his house,

Now when this epistle is read among you, see that it is read also in the church of the Laodiceans, and that you likewise read the epistle from Laodicea. And say to Archippus, "Take heed to the ministry which you have received in the Lord, that you may fulfill it.".

This salutation by my own hand—Paul. Remember my chains. Grace be with you. Amen.

(Colossians 1:1-29, 2:1-23, 3:1-25, 4:1-18).

We have a great cloud of witnesses to confirm the truth that God is in our midst had and has come to live in and among us. The life you keep, the life you live, is the one that matters the most for you and everyone after you.

Remember why we are here. And remind someone else today. By God's grace; His breath is us, we live. Let us praise Him who saves and keeps, with all that we are, in all that we do (Psalm 105:6).

CHAPTER 9

Learning The Welcome

This fearful world has stolen so much from us. The fear of attack from all sides has caused us to put up walls that have made us blind to our most important assets: our faith in love and being loved and loving each other.

We have learned how to take from each other, but the grace of giving back in truth and deed is lost. Certainly, media promotions inspire us to give and to help others in need. Yet in reality, as a defense mechanism, we as a society have stopped reaching out for fear of being taken advantage of because of all the taking in our society and not giving back.

When we do give, we expect a gold star or a special gratuity for something we needed to do anyway. Life and hope have their own rewards.

We are not free to love or build a relationship with God or another person holding onto bitterness and unforgiveness.

A good example of our falling short as a nation, as a society: our past history from the fifties to the seventies. The race riots and peace marches of the fifties. It was just after the second world war. The public call for racial equality heard in our land of the presumed free and home of the brave showed our true heart for justice for all. Our solution: assassinations and beatings, murder, and more humiliation for the black, brown and in between. Our days of struggles just barely easing away from the government camps for Japanese Americans imprisoned for being Japanese during the war against Japan. After the fifties came a wave of feminists taking their complaint to the streets and to D.C., Roe vs. Wade (an excuse to murder our innocent children in the womb) up to present date, we as a society, have slaughtered more babies in the last few decades than all the people who have died in all the wars of modern history combined.

The Vietnam incursion (war)-came by way of L.B.J., just after Nixon was politely urged to leave his office as president of the United States (sort of) America as a nation went ballistic. Riots in the streets. Peace signs on everything everywhere a yellow circle with and an upside down fork could be painted, stamped, or printed in defiance of our American military dying in a land we had no business invading. American flags were burned to our shame as a nation. Bras were burned in the name of female equality and people were trampled and shot in our homeland. Make love not war was plastered, burned into our memories and the paradox of "burn baby burn", screamed in our ears and in the media. Woodstock came and went, a lull in the rage and outburst of hate and utter rebellion. And through it all peace and love was trampled underfoot in the name of civil rights and the pursuit of happiness. All in the aftermath of a civil war over slavery and just prior to this horror, a declaration of independence from the tyranny of English rule. When the smoke cleared along the way, bills in congress were written and signed, laws were passed, reparations put in place for all the damage done; without apology. Racial equality put into law. Sexual equality was declared on paper and enforced. Segregation outlawed in law but not accomplished in the heart. We put all the laws in place to stop the injustices from oppressing this nations populace. But through all the deaths, through all the unjust acts in the name of justice no peace came from the blood that was spilled on our homeland. Nothing became equal for anyone. Homosexuality was and is also being cramed into our right to destroy ourselves attached to the feminist movement; which has nothing to do sexual equality at all. The freedom for all was turned into bondage and liberty and justice for all the reserved for those who could afford it. With all our "i's" dotted and "t's" crossed we haven't changed a thing for the better.

The older generation of present day, who were the younger generation of those inglorious years of America at our worst, have forgotten the struggles of the injustices having settled into the entitlements that our society affords us, stepping aside from mentoring the younger generation of today. Men have bowed out to let the women "do it"; whatever..... The women of this nation do not have sexual equality in light of the American dream. Instead the female person has been made a target of male aggression.

The seventies have returned. The seeds sown of the fifties and sixties and seventies have come back on us.

As a people, as a nation; together we need to turn to the "In God We Trust", and find the way back to our heavenly Father through His Son Jesus. Jesus told us and tells us again how we may return to the heavenly Father's welcome. It is to do the work of God, "To believe in the one whom God sent.". God's welcome is in His Son Jesus and is found when we surrender to Jesus and proclaim Him Lord and King of heaven and earth and all creation. His leading words are found in the gospel according to Matthew the disciple:

One day, amid thousands of people who had followed Jesus because of the many miracles He had performed, He chose a place on the mountainside that overlooked the valley filled with the people looking up at Him. This is the record of the event:

"And seeing the multitudes, He went up on a mountain, and when He was seated His disciples came to Him. Then He opened His mouth and taught them, saying:

Blessed are the poor in spirit, For theirs is the kingdom of heaven. Blessed are those who mourn, For they shall be comforted. Blessed are the meek, For they shall inherit the earth. Blessed are those who hunger and thirst for righteousness, For they shall be filled.

Blessed are the merciful, For they shall obtain mercy.

Blessed are the pure in heart, For they shall see God. Blessed are the peacemakers,

For they shall be called sons of God. Blessed are those who are persecuted for righteousness' sake,

For theirs is the kingdom of heaven.

Blessed are you when they revile and persecute you, and say all kinds of evil against you falsely for My sake, Rejoice and be exceedingly glad, for great is your reward in heaven, for so they persecuted the prophets who were before you. "You are the salt of the earth; but if the salt loses its flavor, how shall it be seasoned? It is then good for nothing but to be thrown out and trampled underfoot by men.

You are the light of the world. A city that is set on a hill cannot be hidden. Nor do they light a lamp and put it under a basket, but on a lamp stand, and it gives light to all who are in the house. Let your light so shine before men, that they may see your good works and glorify your Father in heaven.". (Matthew 5:1-16)

The words Jesus spoke to His disciples and the crowd near Him and in the valley below were words of power found only in our surrender to Him. He is God's welcome to us. As we choose to walk in darkness and hide in disobedience we are far from His welcome. Jesus is the Light of heaven that stepped into our darkness to show us the way back through Him to the Father, who gives us power to be called His son's and daughter's of God. God in His grace has restored our welcome through His Son, the Great Shepherd, the Holy Lamb of God. There is no halfway in this matter of accepting Him as Lord and King. Receive the Son of God and live or reject the Son of God and die and die again. God made us to love Him. He loved us first. He loves us more than we can possible think or imagine. God is a holy God and His people are called to be a holy people, to be like Him, in all ways, in all things, a people of light with no darkness in us. Our relationship of holiness with our heavenly Father is what we had before sin and shame entered our soul, through the fall of the first man and woman. The relationship of holiness returns to us through Jesus His Son, the Holy Lamb of God; too every person created, born and yet to born.

Looking on the face of Jesus through faith we see the face of God and live and live again. Through the Light of His love our sight is restored and we can look on each other without fear, as well. As we welcome Jesus into our day, He leads us into the gift of the welcome to life and love to begin again with God and with each other. The welcome is the manifestation far beyond us, but through Jesus the Great Shepherd we walk with Him and talk with Him in heavenly places where He is, through faith, walking in His presence in the light of His welcome.

How this works is something He teaches us in our pauses, highs and lows, and in the "in betweens" of day to day. In the light of His love we can see the world more clearly. Remember many more son's and daughter's have yet arrived to be part of such a great cloud of witnesses. So continue sharing His welcome. We cannot stare at the problem to find the solution. We need to keep our eyes on Jesus, the Great Shepherd, who leads us. So take a breath. Step back and see the wonder of His love unfolding before us.

Like you, I am learning my heavenly Father's welcome again and again. And how to share His welcome with the people that cross my path. I do have to be wise though. When I see a broken soul my first response is to fix the hurt, but I am learning that Jesus my Savior is the fixer.

Also like you I see my face in the mirror with complete honesty seeing all the imperfections but then I look beyond my image and see the son I am in the Son of God, Jesus. I reflect on the wonderful grace His welcome affords to me. His welcome to me just as I am. And by the power of his welcome I am learning to accept others just as they are.

The gift of the welcome is free to all who may come and be set free. It is our choice to live and live again or die, that is in our hands. When we receive our heavenly Father's welcome, in the person of His Son Jesus, the person of Jesus wells up inside us like a spring of living water and flows out to others who draw near to us as we draw nearer to Jesus.

Those who hunger and thirst for His righteousness shall be filled, just as He promised. Yes there is a lot of angry people in the world that we will cross paths with, but God's welcome is far Greater and more powerful than all that are in this world. Take hold of the Great Shepherd's hand and take hold of the one with the greatest need and nearest us and walk into the light of God's awesome love.

A self-assessment is a good practice as you walk in faith with the Lord Jesus, walking with others. We need to let go of our toys that we don't really need. Our treasures are where our heart is. By faith put your treasures in a place where they won't rust and get stolen away by a thief. How do we do this? Seek first the kingdom of God and His righteousness and all the things you need will be added to you here on earth and into eternity. The real treasure is God's awesome presence and the company of others who love Him. The best way to keep adding to your account is to keep the welcome going,

It may seem such a small thing, this welcome, but it is the crucial missing part in all relationships of broken people. A shared welcome with God to each other gives strength to the weak and hurting and the lost. The power of the welcome was way before there was time. When God the Father, God the Son and God His Holy Spirit viewing the visions of creation, of man and woman and all that was going to be, in my gut, I believe that the welcome was the first thing created, making way for everyone and everything that would be created, and born to live, and follow to take part in the awesome mystery of God's love story.

To bring Americans back to each other the foundation of a personal relationship with God and our neighbor must be re-established. A shared smile when passing someone. An extended helping hand. A pause of unspoken concern at the side of another person at just the right time. We need to remember each other in the moment in the day to store up a few more treasures of the heart and mind. Everybody has the power of the welcome but it is only powerful if we give it away. Just put the welcome mat at your feet as you go and live.

Welcome mats used to be on everybody's doorstep. It greeted the person coming and going with a welcome of hospitality and the benefits of the hospitality within the home and those who dwelt there. There is a wonderful thing about welcome mats, they are a lot like our laps. We don't really notice them until we stop to rest in the company of others.

God made the welcome so no one would ever have to walk alone. No matter where we are or where we go, someone would always be there with us. No one was meant to walk alone. Our heavenly Father, Jesus, the Great Shepherd, and His Holy Spirit are always near. Heavens welcome resounds throughout the earth and all creation, to all who stop to listen for the voice of love, the voice of God our Father in heaven. The Great Shepherd is calling now. He calls to you to come and rest. Just as light is the densest matter in all creation, and love the mightiest power of all, the welcome is the cornerstone of all relationships with God and with each other, and all that is. God put it there.

It shines and sings sweetly, calling to all who may come, who are lost and broken to enter.

The state of our being lies in the way we walk in this paradox of light and darkness. How we approach the giving and taking of life determines our ability to love others and be loved by them. In our day to day, moment to moment, we so often forget our important relationship with the invisible world that watches every move we make, that can only be seen through the eyes of faith as we walk in the love of Jesus the Christ. If we do not take the time to see what is right in front of us, right now, it could be gone forever and never come about to be seen again, in the same way. Life is always changing but God shall always remain the same. In order to grow we need to learn how to be a part of the mystery of God's love. The want of greed and lust leads us to isolation and death. The miracle of God's love is just one whisper away. As we walk in perfect love all fear will be gone in living life walking in our hope restored through The Son of God.

In our haste we rush right past the comfort song that other people are singing to us as we cross paths with them. The welcome is where you are and where you are going. The welcome is God's Son, Jesus. Again I say that Jesus is the Door, the Way back to the Father in heaven, (John 10: 1-17).

God has prepared special moments for each of us to show His love to us. God is not a respecter of persons, that is, God loves us all equally and rewards us openly in regard to our choices and who we choose to serve. The invincible thing about God is He knows what we need long before we ask for it. God is God. He knows everything. But He likes to surprise His children with wonderful things in the moment at any moment. Living by the water, I have seen many beautiful manifestations of clouds, wind, water and light. God is so awesome in the way He expresses Himself to His creation. I marvel at His creation because it confirms His promise to never leave us. We are always and forever remembered.

One day, I was driving to Alanson, to home. Lori's caregiver had to leave at a certain time. It was my time to return and carry on. The Little Traverse Bay area is constantly changing with lake effect weather patterns. You can see waterspouts gracefully dance across the wide bay, and the clouds and rainfall are majestic.

And the rainbows can leave you speechless. As I drove down past the bay, I noticed a double rainbow of yellow, orange, pink, green, and perfect blue. I watched the rainbows as I drove looking for the end of the arc. I saw that one of the rainbows ended on the hood of my blue Chevy Impala. I smiled and wept to think just how much God loved me.

The fact that the rainbow was resting on my car is something I have never seen before or since. I have lived by or near the water all my life, and I have seen many rainbows. This rainbow stayed with me until my view of the bay ended.

So many times, I had felt isolated as my wife and I worked through her end-of life care. It seemed that everybody had forgotten us in our journey towards her end. Perhaps people were afraid or just gave us up. Perhaps they felt there was nothing more they could do.

That day, my heavenly Father remembered me in what I needed. He reminded me that under every leaf, in every drop of rain, in every star, on every mountain, in every grain of sand, His love shines for you and me. Every whisper and blast of the wind sings His love songs. His goodness rings loud and strong and constant. His welcome of love is written on the smallest atom and greatest galaxy equally. "Welcome home! I've missed you, my child!", are the words He writes across the sky.

His only request of us is that we remember Him in all we do and say for Him and to and for each other. To remind each other that He is always there waiting for us to return back to Him to walk with Him and talk with Him to begin again. He is our Father in heaven. We are His creation. God wants us back.

CHAPTER 10

Finding The Inner Child

In Matthew's gospel, Jesus put a seemingly impossible stop sign in our face.

"At that time the disciples came to Jesus, saying, "Who then is greatest in the kingdom of heaven?"

Then Jesus called a little child to Him, set him in the midst of them, and said, "Assuredly, I say to you, unless you are converted and become as little children, you will by no means enter the kingdom of heaven. Therefore whoever humbles himself as this little child is the greatest in the kingdom of heaven. Whoever receives one little child like this in My name receives Me.". (Matthew 18: 1-5)

We will always be someone's child no matter how old we get. And the simple truth of our existence is that we will always need someone bigger, stronger and smarter. The state of our life is such that our body was made so frail and our life is so very fragile. Going back to the beginning of conception, God breathed His life into us. In our mother's body we trusted in God and our mothers care to be complete in our full development, with all of our fingers and toes and cute little nose in place. And though we were born into sin through the fall of the first man and woman that is not the end of the story, it is only the beginning. For at the time of our birth we were completely dependent. Always will be. No matter how big and strong or small we grow into we will always need God our heavenly Father, God, Jesus the Son, and His Holy Spirit; and each other. Remember we are called Adam (man and woman). A name taken from the root word meaning clay or dust. We are all the same height before our Creator. A pile of beloved dust. We quickly grow to full stature in the very short time of fifteen to twenty years in body. But in mind it takes a bit longer, a lifetime. Ironically we never actually grow up until we find our inner child, the small person that lives deep in our heart. In the cockles of our being they wait to see the wonder of all that is; to step unto the light and live again, twirling about with a gazillion questions. The questions of who we are, who we belong to, and where we are going just out there. God put these questions in place to help bring us back to Him through His Son, Jesus the Christ. And by His Holy Spirit living in us we will have the power to walk through the clutter of this life. We may try to fill the void that exists, but we will only further smother the waiting child inside us all the more doing things our own way.

But in every heart there is crack of light in the door that shall always remain, His Truth, that will help lead us back to walking and talking with our heavenly Father as it was in the beginning. Through this crack of light in our soul we have a way to reach through the darkness to take hold of the Light of the world, Jesus the Son of God, The light of Heaven and earth, Lord of all of creation. And if we just reach one more inch farther, in faith, we will find His hand reaching back to us, to pull us through the darkness and into the light of His love to dwell in His heart for always.

In our hearts God put the void to send us searching for more, which leads us back to Him. A trail of bread crumbs. Jesus said that unless we become as little children we cannot see the kingdom of God nor can we enter therein. A simple faith. Our heavenly Father said it. We believe it and take His hand and walk as He leads us. As adults we become calloused. We need to see the result before we will accept the gift that life presents in the moment. Until we let our inner child step into the Light we are dead in our sin and blind. Yet and still our heavenly Father keeps reaching back waiting for our return to come back home to Him. Our sin is great but His love is greater. He loved us first.

Because of our sinful nature we need incentives to help us see, to return back to God. I say it again, He loved us first. His mercy is beyond the limits of all we could dream.

For the human brain to get the signal that there is problem, God put a brake in the system; in our body and soul. With this hook of preservation in place we live this moment to pause and consider our middle and end and what is beyond our last breath. The information that flows into our eye gate and ear gate greatly effects our decisions in how we live and die. The things we hear and see cannot be taken for granted for one moment. To live is our goal. To live well we must be aware of the attack on our soul and take heart to stand in the Lord's care. Be careful little eyes what you see.....be careful little ears what you hear for the Father up above is standing near in love. It is our sinful nature that we resist instruction. Men, we know that the instructions are there for a reason. But as men go, before entering the project we set aside the instructions first.

The instruction manual is there for a reason. That left over screw and nut and bolt will come back at us. But God our heavenly Father has a way of getting us back to the original plan of the restoration of our life with Him and the healing of the family. His design will be as He said it would be. PERIOD!! Be assured that God is very near to us always. When we fall down He is right there to pick us up in love. And when we are down all we need to do to see Him is to look up to see the cross and take His hand of mercy, to begin again. Realize this: we can do nothing without Him. If you want to find out where you are when you are lost, instead of going around in circles a dozen times, stop and see where you started from and start again.

The Light we are admonished to seek is Jesus the Light of the World, the Glory of Heaven. In Him, we will find our way back to our Father in heaven. Our return to His fellowship may be through places we thought we would never go, doing things we thought we would never do. But remember, this is His plan. When we see through the eyes of faith, in Jesus our Lord and Savior, we will find the inner child and live again and again, as He leads us into becoming the beautiful creation He meant for us to be. And yes we may hit the same sore spot a few times but along the way we will discover that the journey back to Him is not just for us. As we walk with Him on the way, we shine His light of life and hope as a son or daughter called by His name.

The specific term of the enlightenment that we seek is the state of being born again. What does being born again really mean? Let us ponder the depth of this question as we read the words of the conversation that Jesus had with His friend Nicodemus:

"There was a man of the Pharisees named Nicodemus, a ruler of the Jews. This man came to Jesus by night and said to Him, "Rabbi, we know that You are a teacher come from God; for no one can do these signs that You do unless God is with him.

Jesus answered and said to him, "Most assuredly, I say to you, unless one is born again, he cannot see the kingdom of God.".

Nicodemus said to Him, "How can a man be born when he is old? Can he enter a second time into his(her) mother's womb and be born?".

Jesus answered, "Most assuredly, I say to you, unless one is born of water and the Spirit, he cannot enter the kingdom of God. That which is born of the flesh is flesh, and that which is born of the Spirit is spirit. Do not marvel that I said to you, 'You must be born again.' The wind blows where it wishes, and you hear the sound of it, but cannot tell where it comes from and where it goes. So is everyone who is born of the Spirit.".

Nicodemus answered and said to Him, "How can these things be?".

Jesus answered and said to him, "Are you the teacher of Israel, and do not know these things? Most assuredly, I say to you, We speak what We know and testify what We have seen, and you do not receive Our witness. If I have told you earthly things and you do not believe, how will you believe if I tell you heavenly things? No one has ascended to heaven but He who came down from heaven, that is, the Son of Man who is in heaven. And as Moses lifted up the serpent in the wilderness, even so must the Son of Man be lifted up, that whoever believes in Him should not perish but have eternal life. For God so loved the world that He gave His only begotten Son, that whoever believes in Him should not perish but have everlasting life. For God did not send His Son into the world to condemn the world, but that the world through Him might be saved.

He who believes in Him is not condemned; but he who does not believe is condemned already, because he has not believed in the name of the only begotten Son of God. And this is the condemnation, that the light has come into the world, and men loved darkness rather than light, because their deeds were evil. For everyone practicing evil hates the light and does not come to the light, lest his deeds should be exposed. But he who does the truth comes to the light, that his deeds may be clearly seen, that they have been done in God.".

"After these things Jesus and His disciples came into the land of Judea, and there He remained with them and baptized.", (John 3:1-22).

We wonder just how Nicodemus answered Jesus. It is not noted. I imagine Jesus putting His hand on this dear friend's shoulder, a man he may have played with when they were boys, and smiling as Nicodemus stood dumbfounded at the thought of being reborn. The man that Nicodemus presumed Him to be was not the same person Jesus always was, the same person was Jesus the Christ long before time was, so let us address the question with Nicodemus. How then shall a man (or woman), be born again shall he (or she), enter into his(hers) mother's womb a second time when he (or she) is old?

A dear friend of mine, a doctor of medicine named Robin Bachelor, once asked me where I came from.

I smiled. "Well, there was a seed..." I didn't finish my comment because it would have ruined the punch line. He just smiled and I said, "Well, you asked.", I replied.

All life begins with a seed. Each seed when it is planted grows into what it started to be. But if it does not germinate it suffers a kind of permanent death if it is not allowed to change to unfold to take root and grow up and out. The crack of His light in our heart, His seed of truth that God is God and we are not: that God put into our soul, heart, and mind. We need His Living Water, The Word of God; and the Light of heaven; Jesus His Son; the light of His love to grow into the beautiful creation He made us to be. The child within us waits to walk in the light of His presence and know His loving embrace.

We will hear many voices calling out to us but there is only one voice that can save us: the gentle awesome voice of the Great Shepherd; Jesus our Savior, Emanuel-God with us, Jesus the Christ. As we turn around into His presence that little crack of light becomes wider and wider and brighter as the door to our heart opens up one small miracle at a time. As we reach up in faith His hand reaches back and He draws us into His wonder of heaven on earth. In the warmth of His love, the child asleep in the darkness of sin and death awakens into heavens Light. Then His Holy Spirit comes into our soul, heart and mind and we breath His life and live again and again as the darkness melts away as the snow on a warm sunny day.

So how does all this happen? How can you become born again? Raise your hands, close your eyes, and surrender to the one who is bigger, stronger and smarter than you, and as you stand at the cliffs edge of change, understanding three things: When you ask, God will answer you 'yes, no, or 'wait. To be loved and to love, get ready for change.

Most important, God is a good God. He wants the best for us in all things in this life and the life to come. Psalm 23 explains in depth of the wonderful life God our heavenly Father has in store for us now and for always:

"The Lord is my shepherd; I shall not want. He makes me to lie down in green pastures; He leads me beside the still waters.

He restores my soul; He leads me in the paths of righteousness For His name's sake.

Yea, though I walk through the valley of the shadow of death, I will fear no evil; For You are with me; Your rod and Your staff, they comfort me. You prepare a table before me in the presence of my enemies; You anoint my head with oil; My cup runs over. Surely goodness and mercy shall follow me All the days of my life; And I will dwell in the house of the Lord Forever." (Psalm 23: 1-6).

Everybody presumes that the valley of the shadow of death is somewhere down a gloomy road we will see physically, and on occasion, it may turn out that way. But most of the way back to fellowship with Him starts at the crack of light that opens our soul to walk in the light of His love. As the door to the soul opens to the light of truth, the child hidden in the dark steps out of a prison. The walk back is a journey through all the things and people who clutter; that obstruct the joy, peace, and love that ought to be where the dark places are.

The paths are the many places He will guide us through into and onto the other side. We walk in this protection of His love and care: His rod and His staff they comfort us. He is The Bread of Life and The Lion of Judah. He leads us with His hand upon us and is so close His voice is near and dear to our ear, as He leads us through the darkness of this world every step we take with Him the light of His presence becomes brighter and brighter. As you walk with Him keep your eyes looking at Him only and remember: He will never leave you nor forsake you. And though troubles may come and go in this life; Jesus is Lord over it all. He is the King of heaven and earth and all will answer to Him. On our journey through the valleys of this life we may stumble and fall but remain calm and rest in His care and just keep your eyes on Him. The Great Shepherd knows all of your life even before your conception and He knows how to get you through the difficult times and the hurt, you may experience through the trial of life as you go forward into the mystery of His love and majesty. The power of the lust of the eyes and the lust of the flesh and the pride of life loses its grip on us one step at time with each step of faith that we take. It is by the power of His name that we live, to be called the sons and daughters of God to His leading by His Holy Spirit in us.

There is no one righteous; we have all sinned and come short of the glory of God (Romans 3:10, 3:23). The Lord God is the God of joy. His joy is the source of our strength to carry on (Nehemiah 8: 10; Psalm 51: 12; John 1, 17:13).

Our inner child was meant to see the happiness of love and know peace and safety. Like any child, we need the secure feeling of knowing where home is and that at any time, we have a place to turn and someone to turn to in sorrow and rejoicing.

Our purpose in being born again is to know our child within and to live (Romans 8: 15; John 4:23).

Jesus is The Way, The truth, and The Life, Light of Heaven, God the everlasting Father, The Prince of Peace. He is our Helper in the present time of need. As the Great Shepherd, Jesus goes before, us and has our back as He hedges us in like a cocoon, His cubicle of love. Where His Holy Spirit leads us we follow as His own (2 Corinthians 6: 18, I Corinthians 2: 10, John 14:6, 2 Corinthians 3:19).

Learning again to be His child is not burdensome (John 5:3). As we awake we arise unto Him each day that is given to us. His love. His majesty. His calming voice leading us into His rest (Matthew 11:25-30).

Everything we expected from God is all wrong because our Father is more than we could ever imagine Him to be. He is everything good, loving, and merciful. In the pause between faith and eternity, we walk the path of His blessings and empowerment and become His sons and daughters.

When we are born again, we receive a clearer view of our lives and the life to come through the eyes of His Spirit. We see ourselves as we were and what He has made us to be just as we were meant to be---His image of love.

The journey we take to find ourselves in Him is not far---just one little step and another and another until we see the other side of the valley He leads us through. The Lord God is omniscient, omnipresent, an eternal being who is in all things at all times. In His loving mercy, He became dimensional so we could see Him as we see each other (Genesis 1: 1-31, 2:1 25; John I : 1-18; Psalm 139:1-18; Revelation 1:8; John 6:46). He created a physical hand for us to hold. His name is Jesus, His only begotten Son (l Corinthians 15:39-49). With Jesus in us, by His Holy Spirit, we are made His, as we are in Him. And because He is in us, we can know Him and know each other by His Holy Spirit. We are the body of Christ.

Finding the inner child in us is a lifetime adventure full of thrills, spills, chills, and dipsy-doodles. But in all things Jesus leads us as we walk with Him and talk with Him. He is always with us. His promise to us, "Light is sown for the righteous". He is above us. Around us. Behind us. His Holy Spirit lives in us. Our job as sons and daughters is to follow His leading, to serve Him serving each other and to do the work of God, "To believe on the One whom God sent". We were born again as children meant to know the heavenly Father. It is our job as His sons and daughters to get to know Him and walk with Him through everything in life. Everything! There are no secrets with God. To walk in His perfect love is to walk without fearing of being exposed for who we are, right where we are, just as we are. So walk without fear of rejection as you remain in His love and know beyond any doubt you will always be loved no matter what (Romans 8:3739).

As we walk, Jesus leading the way, with His hand upon us; we will expose the darkness of this world that it will flee so the lost may come and be set free to live again in the Light of His love. We will see as He sees and hear as He hears, being with Him in heavenly places, as heaven has come to earth through Him.

The child you are inside has waited a lifetime to be rejoined with our heavenly Father's company. It will take the rest of your lifetime to learn who we are in Him. All of life and creation move and breath in Him and by His gift of grace we are His as we turn to Him and get lost in His love and love Him back.

CHAPTER 11

Keeping Watch

Let's begin with Jesus' words regarding end times:

"Now as He sat on the Mount of Olives, the disciples came to Him privately, saying, "Tell us, when will these things be? And what will be the sign of Your coming, and of the end of the age?".

And Jesus answered and said to them: "Take heed that no one deceives you. For many will come in My name, saying, I am the Christ, and will deceive many. And you will hear of wars and rumors of wars. See that you are not troubled; for all these things must come to pass, but the end is not yet. For nation will rise against nation, and kingdom against kingdom.

"And there will be famines, pestilences, and earthquakes in various places. All these are the beginning of sorrows."

Then they will deliver you up to tribulation and kill you, and you will be hated by all nations for My name's sake. And then many will be offended, will betray one another, and will hate one another. Then many false prophets will rise up and deceive many. And because lawlessness will abound, the love of many will grow cold. But he who endures to the end shall be saved. And this gospel of the kingdom will be preached in all the world as a witness to all the nations, and then the end will come."

"Therefore when you see the 'abomination of desolation,' spoken of by Daniel the prophet, standing in the holy place, (whoever reads, let him understand), "then let those who are in Judea flee to the mountains. Let him who is on the housetop not go down to take anything out of his house, And let him who is in the field not go back to get his clothes. But woe to those who are pregnant and to those who are nursing babies in those days! And pray that your flight may not be in winter or on the Sabbath. For then there will be great tribulation, such as has not been since the beginning of the world until this time, no, nor ever shall be. And unless those days were shortened, no flesh would be saved; but for the elects sake those days will be shortened."

"Then if anyone says to you, Look, here is the Christ!' or (There!' do not believe it. For false christs and false prophets will rise and show great signs and wonders to deceive, if possible, even the elect. See, I have told you beforehand."

"Therefore if they say to you, Look, He is in the desert!' do not go out; or "Look, He is in the inner rooms!' do not believe it. For as the lightning comes from the east and flashes to the west, so also will the coming of the Son of Man be. For wherever the carcass is, there the eagles will be gathered together."

"Immediately after the tribulation of those days the sun will be darkened, and the moon will not give its light; the stars will fall from heaven, and the powers of the heavens will be shaken. Then the sign of the Son of Man will appear in heaven, and then all the tribes of the earth will mourn, and they will see the Son of Man coming on the clouds of heaven with power and great glory. And He will send His angels with a great sound of a trumpet, and they will gather together His elect from the four winds, from one end of heaven to the other."

"Now learn this parable from the fig tree: When its branch has already become tender and puts forth leaves, you know that summer is near. So you also, when you see all these things, know that it is near—at the doors! Assuredly, I say to you, this generation will by no means pass away till all these things take place. Heaven and earth will pass away, but My words will by no means pass away.".

"But of that day and hour no one knows, not even the angels of heaven, but my Father only.

But as the days of Noah were, so also will the coming of the Son of Man be. For as in the days before the flood, they were eating and drinking, marrying and giving in marriage, until the day that Noah entered the ark, and did not know until the flood came and took them all away, so also will the coming of the Son of Man be. Then two men will be in the field: one will be taken and the other left. Two women will be grinding at the mill: one will be taken and the other left. Watch therefore, for you do not know what hour your Lord is coming. But know this, that if the master of the house had known what hour the thief would come, he would have watched and not allowed his house to be broken into. Therefore you also be ready, for the Son of Man is coming at an hour you do not expect.".

"Who then is a faithful and wise servant, whom his master made ruler over his household, to give them food in due season? Blessed is that servant whom his master, when he comes, will find so doing. Assuredly, I say to you that he will make him ruler over all his goods. But if that evil servant says in his heart, 'My master is delaying his coming, ' and begins to beat his fellow servants, and to eat and drink with the drunkards, the master of that servant will come on a day when he is not looking for him and at an hour that he is not aware of, and will cut him in two and appoint him his portion with the hypocrites. There shall be weeping and gnashing of teeth." (Matthew 24: 3-51).

Jesus rose from the grave on the third day just as He had promised. He walked with the people and talked with the people to complete the comfort He promised them. Then he ascended to the Lord God in heaven to finish the rest of His story, but before He left, He gathered them together:

"And Jesus came and spoke to them, saying, "All authority has been given to Me in heaven and on earth. Go therefore and make disciples of all the nations, baptizing them in the name of the Father and of the

Son and of the Holy Spirit, teaching them to observe all things that I have commanded you; and Lo, I am with you always, even to the end of the age." (Matthew 28: 18-20).

Also in the gospel according to Mark:

"Now the Pharisees, who were lovers of money, also heard all these things, and they derided Him. And He said to them, "You are those who justify yourselves before men, but God knows your hearts. For what is highly esteemed among men is an abomination in the sight of God."

"The law and the prophets were until John. Since that time the kingdom of God has been preached, and everyone is pressing into it. And it is easier for heaven and earth to pass away than for one tittle of the law to fail.". (Luke 16: 14-17).

In Psalm 91, our Lord and Savior admonished us:

"He who dwells in the secret place of the Most High shall abide under the shadow of the Almighty. I will say of the Lord, "He is my refuge and my fortress; My God, in Him I will trust." Surely He shall deliver you from the snare of the fowler and from the perilous pestilence. He shall cover you with His feathers, and under His wings you shall take refuge; His truth shall be your shield and

[b]buckler. You shall not be afraid of the terror by night, nor of the arrow that flies by day, nor of the pestilence that walks in darkness, nor of the destruction that lays waste at noonday.

A thousand may fall at your side, and ten thousand at your right hand; But it shall not come near you. Only with your eyes shall you look, and see the reward of the wicked.

Because you have made the Lord, who is my refuge, even the Most High, your dwelling place, no evil shall befall you, nor shall any plague come near your dwelling; For He shall give His angels charge over you, to keep you in all your ways. In their hands they shall bear you up, lest you dash your foot against a stone. You shall tread upon the lion and the cobra, the young lion and the serpent you shall trample underfoot.

"Because he has set his love upon Me, therefore I will deliver him; I will set him on high, because he has known My name. He shall call upon Me, and I will answer him; I will be with him in trouble; I will deliver him and honor him. With long life I will satisfy him, and show him My salvation.". (Psalm 91 : 1-16)

The people who need to hear the good news of Jesus all have names and places where they live; they have cultural heritages that can be open doors for them to hear the gospel. Going into all the world is the way to love people where they are, at home, in the place where they find comfort. Jesus makes His home in everyone's heart just as they are where they are. Bring the presence of God's house to them in their cultures and times. The love words of Jesus are the same for everyone. His word is written in hearts already; we just need to speak the Word of life to wake them to the truth. We are to be all things to all people that we might win some (l Corinthians 9: 19).

The church, the body of Christ, is in the limelight of the world's constant skepticism. Even though they are walking in darkness, they can see the real deal or a phony faith. The people all around us are scared to death about the uncertainty in the world. They are looking for answers. We are a light to the world in Christ; what shall we answer them? What shall we do during the brief time we are here?

The words of the Lord that were spoken to Solomon can give us a place where we can begin as a people.

"Then the Lord appeared to Solomon by night, and said to him: "I have heard your prayer, and have chosen this place for Myself as a house of sacrifice. When I shut up heaven and there is no rain, or command the locusts to devour the land, or send pestilence among My people, if My people who are called by My name will humble themselves, and pray and seek My face, and turn from their wicked ways, then I will hear from heaven, and will forgive their sin and heal their land. Now My eyes will be open and My ears attentive to prayer made in this place. For now I have chosen and sanctified this house, that My name may be there forever; and My eyes and My heart will be there perpetually.". (2 Chronicles 7:12-16).

The church, the body of Christ, is one body with many parts; we need to be the body of Christ as we were called to be as we briefly walk with each other and those who are yet to receive the mark of His love.

We are called by the Holy Spirit of Jesus to walk in the fullness of His gifts made manifest. We are His holy people; we are the holy temple in which He dwells.

To truly appreciate just what that means, we need to look in the Old Testament and rediscover the presence of God working on earth and in whom He put His Spirit to accomplish His intimate and mighty works. In Genesis, the Lord God confirmed our beginning. We were created in His image (Genesis I :26; 2:15-24). His breath of life was put into us to give us His presence of life that we would always live with Him, (Genesis 2: 7). The woman likewise was given the breath of life and was to live forever with the man and the Lord God equal in all things with the man (Genesis 2:22-23).

The man and the woman fell to sin and shame (Genesis 3: I -24.) though His eternal Spirit left the man and the woman, His presence did not leave the earth ; He had a plan of salvation to redeem them (Genesis 3:15).

The Lord God's favor was granted to His chosen people to carry out His plan of salvation through the lineage of those he called to continue in His grace and good pleasure (Genesis 6:5-22, 7:1-24, 8: 1-22, 9:1-17). An eternal covenant was made by the Lord God with Abraham to fulfill the promise of His plan of redemption (Genesis 12: 1-2). The Messiah's lineage was given to make complete the virgin birth of Jesus from the throne of David, the Lion of Judah, (Genesis 18:1-15. 25: 19-28). The presence of the Lord God was with Jacob who begat Judah, who were the people of the messianic lineage (Genesis 28: 10-22, 29:1-31. 30:1-26). And the completion of the foundation for David's lineage came in God's promise to Jacob at the place called Peniel:

"And he arose that night and took his two wives, his two female servants, and his eleven sons, and crossed over the ford of Jabbok. He took them, sent them over the brook, and sent over what he had. Then Jacob was left alone; and a Man wrestled with him until the breaking of day. Now when He saw that He did not prevail against him, He touched the socket of his hip; and the socket of Jacob's hip was out of joint as He wrestled with him. And He said, "Let Me go, for the day breaks.'

But he said, 'I will not let You go unless You bless me!
So He said to him, "What is your name?"
He said, "Jacob.".

And He said, "Your name shall no longer be called Jacob, but Israel; for you have struggled with God and with men, and have prevailed.

Then Jacob asked, saying, "Tell me Your name, I pray.".

And He said, "Why is it that you ask about My name?". And He blessed him there.

So Jacob called the name of the place Peniel: "For I have seen God face to face, and my life is preserved.". As he crossed over Penuel the sun rose on him, and he limped on his hip.". (Genesis 33: 22-31)

This leads us to the captivity of Joseph and the children of Israel and their exodus from Egypt (Genesis 37:18-28, 39:1-23, 41:33-41, 47:11, 50:22-23, Exodus 2:1-8, 3:1-22, 12:37-50).

The Lord God, who once walked with the man and the woman in the garden of Eden, has always stayed with us; His promise was to bring us back to Him. The children of Israel, after having been led out of Egypt by Moses and Aaron, walked in God's company with His presence in the pillar of smoke by day and the pillar of fire by night with the angel of the Lord (Exodus 14:19).

The I AM who delivered the people of Israel out of the hand of Pharaoh wanted to draw close to His chosen people. On one occasion, He set up a meeting on Mount Sinai so the people could hear Him and know of His love, but they were afraid (Exodus 19:1-24, 20:1821).

Enter the next, the Holiest of Holies and the ark of the covenant and the law and the commandments (Exodus 20:22-26, 21:1-35, 22:1-31, 23:1-33, 25:10-22, 26:1-37, 31:12-18).

Our heavenly father has always loved us. His only desire is to draw us close and keep us near now and forever (John 3:16). His Spirit was in the chosen men and women to be a presence of hope among the chosen people of His pasture.

Thousands of years passed, and many prophets and prophetess were persecuted and died, but the word of promise kept its march through the ages as the presence of the Lord God completed His plan with us (Matthew 1:22-23).

Jesus grew and walked among us talking with us, touching our hearts, healing and speaking the words of His Father the words of light, life, hope and love. He did everything prophesied of Him; He did everything He said He would do.

Before He ascended to heaven, He sent us His Holy Spirit to be with us until the last man and woman has come to know of His love and the gift of salvation through the cross (Luke 24:48, 49; Matthew 28:18-20). The Holy Spirit filled the people in the upper room empowering them to preach the gospel to every creature just as Jesus had commanded. They told the story and of Jesus' great love. And this is the Great Commission: that we love one another as He has always loved us from before the beginning of time to the man and woman's fall to sin and darkness in the garden of Eden to the end of time into eternity. His Love is never failing, His mercy endures forever.

Behold His face as we walk through this age of fulfillment of prophecy. Do not hear the words of this age; hear the voice of the One who speaks from the throne of grace and sits in the mercy seat in heaven. As you follow His leading, take another person's hand and walk into His awesome, loving arms. Never leave His presence.

CHAPTER 12

Are We There Yet?

I cannot speak for anyone but myself in the matters of choice and conscience. There is much I do not understand about a great many things. Yes I have a gazillion questions. Since I saw my first sunrise my thirst for answers has remained overwhelming. I stand in awe as I watch people and plants blossom and grow into the beautiful creation God made them to be.

With each new day given to me the memories of my life and times tickle into the moments. My adventures of water and woods fill my senses. Since the age of a small boy when I caught my first trout I have come to enjoy fishing. With each fish I catch the adrenaline rush is still there. To date I have had many dinners and have learned much about God's creation.

Each season's change is a delight as I view the symphony of colors and living motion and hear the sounds of all the wonder about me. Singing and dancing His majesty breaths in such unfolding mystery. In Autumn the breezes ease through the trees whispering the songs of Summer's passing. The verdant green turned to red and gold, they too sing a tune that woos my soul and mind at the closing of harvest time.

Soon the earth will be neatly tucked under a blanket of white for a much needed nap.

Every creature, raindrop, blade of grass, and flower petal is a story in itself that can be heard only if you stop and listen carefully. You must stop for a while to hear the songs they sing. God put them in place for us to see and hear and know. If you don't listen now, you will miss it, the beauty that they hold in the small places where only a child would think to go. I have written many pieces of literature since age seventeen. I had an angelic visitation when I was about three. Very early, my eyes were opened to things most people miss because they just went to fast on their way by or they just simply lost the appreciation of the awe and wonder of God's handiwork.

It is all there for anyone to see and hear; only one thing is required of us, put aside our expectations and let life be what it was created to be, simple and majestic, just like the One who created it all.

I have been blessed to see many treasures of water, earth, sky and all the things that move in through, or over it all. We are commanded to worship the Lord God Creator, to see His beauty of purity, goodness, and light that shines from heaven and in all that He made. The pleasure of being here on earth is to see His miracles of life and to share in the blessings of His love for us. He made us from the dust. He called everything that exists from out of nothing and made it into something quite wonderful.

Jesus said, "Except you become as little children you cannot enter into the kingdom.". It is through the wonder of the child that emerges from within our hearts and minds that we can see the truth of what is when we step into the light of His love and stay.

To help you understand a child's heart take a walk with a caterpillar and see its journey's to end one story as it changes to begin yet another story. Pause with a flower blossom and revel in the beauty that unfolds and then quickly passes away and see natures requiem of colors that fill the earth with such splendor. You will see with the child's heart and with a child's eyes look up to your heavenly Father and know that you are loved for always.

In my own personal journey of searching out my child's heart I have seen the wonders of seasons change while fishing. One day, I went fishing at Manuka Lake, just outside Gaylord, Michigan. The air was crisp with the heaviness of Fall. The leaves had turned brown. The sleepy trees were preparing for the coming change; they stood bare and whistled as the colder breezes passed over each branch. The summer resorters had gone back to wherever they came from, and the lake lay with barely a ripple The sky was showing the first signs of winter. Streaks of clouds formed like coarse locks of fine, white hair looming overhead. But for the most part, the sky was deep blue.

I was careful not to make much of a fuss as I stepped into the chilling shallows. I waded up to my knees and made a long cast out to where the big autumn blue gills like to hang out. After few minutes, my bobber went down. I retrieved a hand-sized beauty with light-blue sides and a tan belly.

I put it in my fishing bag and cast again. I repeated the joy of reeling in six more big ones. And then there was a sudden change in the air and the sky. A soft overcast came, and light, gentle snow started falling. I listened to the pat...pat of the snowflakes that lightly came to rest upon the surface of the slumbering lake. For about twenty minutes, the world was quite still as the soft blanket of white filled the space all around me. The snow was so thick that I could not see but a couple of feet about me. I closed my eyes as the perfect snowflakes kissed my face for a fleeting moment.

I had to stop fishing, but that was okay. Moments like these are rare as the peace of the earth came for the brief time of here and now. I just kept my eyes closed as I listened to the lake and the snowflakes lightly play the pat...pat that whispered in my ears.

After a while, the snowfall dissipated, and only gray clouds filled in the deep-blue spaces.

The fish quit biting. So I surrendered to the change in the weather, letting and turning to leave. My steps were slow and reverent to keep in time with the mood of the lake and the air and the sky. As I made shore,

I turned to see the beauty to remember the present moment. I wanted to keep the beauty of the autumn serenade unspoiled in my memory.

I have a favorite poem, that I wrote that tells of a morning visit to one of my childhood haunts in another place and time.

On The Rivers way

The phantoms of the morning light rose off the river flow, as the current courses trod along the steady slow.

The cardinal bird greeted day, a tellers tale to sing and celebrated river's song, good news he came to bring.

The quiet air and still dawn, a cast at early morn', I come to cast a line before the earthly yawn.

I pause to wait for trout to rise and meet the dawning day, to sip the fly, to make a run, and play.

With the first of many landed, then I watch the beauty swim and revel in the restful plot letting as I may.

A few will never swim again and many will take flight to live again as day turns into night.

And they shall dream as will I of all the wondcrous sunlite play and treasure all the gems that shine on the rivers way.

The intimate moments like these are far too easily missed in all the hurry as we turn away from seeing all that God has created for us to wonder about.

In this life we measure our success by the things we presume to own, to prove our accomplishments. We work hard to acquire all that we think is important to us. Apart from our relationship with God and with others this stuff is meaningless. The best toys are not the best things for us. If we live to get gain for ourselves it is for nothing.

Where we store up our treasures makes all the difference in our life here and for the rest of the story. Jesus said, "Do not lay up for yourselves treasures on earth, where moth and rust destroy and where thieves break in and steal; but lay up for yourselves treasures in heaven, where neither moth nor rust destroys and where thieves do not break in and steal. For where your treasure is, there your heart will be also.". (Matthew 6: 19-21 NKJV)

The discipline of worshipping the Lord Jesus in spirit and in truth is in the power of choosing to serving the Lord and to surrender your all in service to Him in all things; as we are commanded to worship Him (John 4:23-24).

We need to willfully push away the clutter that we have put into our lives, we must let go of all things that keep us from lifting our hands, eyes, and hearts to give praise to the Lord, who is worthy of all our praise (Hebrews 12:1; Psalm 150:6, 145:10, 34:1).

For you see the measure of our eternal life is in the balance of what remains that passes through His holy fire after all the unimportant stuff is burned away (Malachi 3:2).

The race we run is not one of flesh and blood; it's of the heart and mind and spirit in heavenly places (1 Corinthians 9:24-27). When we're born into this temporary life, we presume this is all there is, and our thoughts lead us in the pursuits of things that will never last the test of truth and love, but that is not the rest of the story. The truth is that we began our life through God's grace.

Every breath is a gift of His mercy.

Everything we experience here on earth is only on loan for a short time to allow us time to repent of our sin and turn to Him and run into His open arms and stay. The beginning of our story started in the garden of Eden on earth and ended with the our fall into sin and shame. The rest of our story starts with a cross and a welcome from The Great Shepherd Jesus the Christ as we are ushered into eternal fellowship with Him by our surrender to His love and if we do not surrender to the King of Kings and Lord of Lords-King of heaven earth; we will only know the fruit of denial of His gift of grace and we shall know hell and eternal damnation. We were created in Creator God's images and He calls us back to fellowship to Him through His Son Jesus the Christ. It is that simple. It is that wonderful to walk and talk with our heavenly Father once again. To better appreciate our beginnings let us understand that beginning of the story of the first beginning of our life.

We measure mental development by our length of focus. An infant has the attention span of about thirty seconds. A toddler about two minutes or less. A child age four, about two minutes or more. From age four to about age eight, the time increases to about five minutes or less. At age eight to thirteen five minutes to about ten minutes. In the teen years our attention span does not increase much beyond the ten minutes. After twenty years of age and for the remainder of our adult life our focus is between fifteen and twenty minutes, at best, for most people. To keep our focus on one subject at a time much interaction is required to keep us on the subject at present.

It takes four seconds for sexual attraction to occur. Twenty five seconds to conceive a child and a lifetime to discover who the person is to appreciate their being here. We measure our arrival in this life by the time it takes to come to a destination. Seconds, minutes, hours, days, and years are not the way God designed us. Our original created being lives moment by moment so that we will live step by step with God and with each other.

The classic comment of "Are we there yet?" is the constant state of human consciousness.

God gives us a right and left and up and down, an in and out to help us have a sense of direction. Where we began was walking with God our heavenly Father in the moment. This world that we see is a reflection of the spirit world that our physical eyes cannot see. Everything that happens starts in the heavenly places before the throne of God. We live, breath, walk and talk in the presence of God who dearly loves us. He is always near, always was. He is where we are going and to whom we go. Our destination. In our blindness at our conception we begin thinking that we are alone, but the still small voice of God whispers softly speaking to us with the very first beating of our heart. When we are born from the womb our journey begins on our way back to His fellowship. Along the way we learn our place in the community of our people to begin knowing our place in the heavenly community. We have two gifts that are ours. A name and a choice. And so the story goes to do and obey our heavenly Father or to disobey and rebel against His law of love and remain walking in the darkness dying inside our heart and mind. We have community so that we are not alone so that we can learn that someone has always been there who has always loved us. The lesson: that we cannot live in this life and make it on our own. We will always need someone to get on in this life and all the more we need Jesus the Christ to get on into eternity; He is the only way to the Father above. This is the story of heavens grace. This I know to be true. In our daily lives, there will always be laundry and dishes and work and bills. We will try to do it all on our own, but we will fail. And when we fall all we need to do is to look up into our heavenly Father's eyes through Jesus His Son and find a friend who will never leave us nor forsake us. In answer to our question, "Are we there yet?", consider the other questions of our existence: "Where are you in relation to God and other people?, Are you away from them because of indifference? Are you lost and isolated because of your choices?".

Our place in community is defined by the arrival of everyone arriving together at the same place at the same time. When we all get there together we are there. The wonder of community is in the small miracles of the moment.

Do you recall the Tootsie Roll pop commercial? A little boy goes to a wise old owl and asks, "How many licks does it take to get the center of a Tootsie Roll pop?". The wise old owl takes the Tootsie Roll pop in hand and counts, "One, two, three. Crunch! Three.". The narrator breaks in: "And the world may never know.". Well I know. It takes six hundred and thirty-nine licks to get to the center of the tootsie roll pop. It may sound silly to pursue this childish quest, but the answer holds a treasure for life.

The little things of life make all the difference for happiness and wholeness. It is by way of the small things that we can see the bigger picture and the bigger things. We get on by solving one small problem at a time. Only then can we see the family photo of God's creation: God our heavenly Father, Jesus the Christ His Son, His Holy Spirit, the angels of heaven, the men and women made in God's image, and the fallen angels of darkness. The community that is for all eternity. And by His grace we have a place of honor and love if we turn from the darkness and step into the light of His love and stay to love Him back and love each other as we walk and talk with our heavenly Father. The two great commandments are "You shall love Lord your God with all your heart, with all your soul, with all your mind, and with all your strength and You shall love your neighbor as yourself.". (Mark 12:29-31). They are not just words. These are the two commandments upon which all things are founded upon in God's truth and in them we will find life and hope and love and peace and joy. A child's heart is an important teacher in this matter of faith. A toddler can only focus for a very short period of time at a time, but they seek constantly to discover the bigger picture of life. Everyone and everything an unanswered question yet to be known in the moment of finding out. They surrender to the delight of the moment led by someone bigger, stronger, smarter than they are. And so we are His dear children walking and talking with Him on the way back home. To live a life it requires a surrender to the need to be loved and to love God and someone else. To get a hug you give a hug. To share a smile you smile. And to hear a word you listen and then speak. This is how we change a world. Tell a story change a heart and change a world. To see the bigger things change, the little things need to change first. We live how we love. We listen how we speak. And we walk as we are led by the company we keep. All of these define our path into life or our continuation into death and darkness. Along the way the many small miracles become the bread crumbs that lead us back to the path of righteousness and goodness. We are always looking for something in our life to be better and easier. The wonder of these miracles is the change of our heart and mind through Jesus the Christ. This is God's perfect plan. Change will come, count on it. The just shall live by faith. All who worship God are servants unto Him alone. Take comfort in the Lord's presence and leading and rest. For He is ever and always working, putting all of His creation back in line with His restoration plan of salvation. We can work in His plan with Him or work against His plan of salvation. But be warned you will discover how big God is and just how small you are. The invitation to come be a part of His plan is to all who may come just as you are. The only thing in our way is the fear of change. Take comfort in His promise that His love, His perfect love, casts out all fear. I know this first hand to be true. Trust the Lord Jesus from right where you are, right now. Only Jesus the Christ can save you and keep you. Surrender and enter into His rest. You have the opportunity to partake of His welcome into His heart of love while you still have breath before you POOF!".

A day full of little miracles, that is our entire existence in a nutshell. It is all in God's plan of redemption of the man and woman. God put them there to lead us back to His love one step at a time back to Him and to each other. Our focus in our short life is to nurture others while we are being nurtured. There is only on constant in the universe: love. God loves us. He has always loved us and He always will. I know that in this life there is much pain and trouble. It is hard for us to understand when things happen to us and to others. I only know that everything happens for a reason in God's plan of restoration. We may not like the bumps that stop us in our day along the way. This too I know to be true that each stop sign is to direct us to the next destination. Our walk of faith is a mystery unfolding in heavenly places where love, His love, is the singular objective for all things with all things. The trek of this life, it never turns out the way we planned. Each relationship we have with other people is in question. Everyone has free will and it is a hard to say how things will turn out between us and them. We can only know that God will never leave nor forsake us and that everyone who is going to be there will be there with us in the outcome of God's plan for us and them. God's creation can teach us of His wonder and beauty, but it is God who makes it beautiful. All things live in a breath by His grace alone. When you and I see a thing it is not the thing we see by itself. It is a reflection of God's love for us. When we see His creation through the eyes of Jesus the Christ His glory is revealed in all His goodness and glory. Everywhere we look there is a signature of His love. As we walk with Jesus we learn how to live again and we will arrive right on time, every time in His time.

We have arrived when we see our Father's good pleasure and know His perfect peace. So many people think that our job well done can only be heard at the end of our life after our last breath but in truth our 'job well done child' we will hear every step of the way till the time we cross over into the land of eternal light. If we do not stop to hear His words of comfort and good pleasure in every moment, as He leads us, we are missing the true delight of His presence in our life. God does what pleases Him. It pleases Him to bless His children with peace and comfort and the joy of knowing that He is well pleased with us in our obedience to His words. His words of love. Our entrance into His fellowship is the completion of a journeys end to begin again. As we serve Him in serving each other we discover just exactly what His good pleasure is: for the body of Christ, the people of light born again; to be one of mind, heart and spirit just as the Father, the Son, and the Spirit are one. The song verse, which is not a bible verse, states that they will know we are christians by our love: this states it well. We will be known as we are known. We are here for just a short time. We need to make the best of our time while we are here. The gift of today is but a moment and then we POOF! How we live and how we die and to whom we live unto makes all the difference between heaven and hell. You have this moment to choose whom you will serve: God through Jesus His Son, the Christ; or the sinful flesh and this dark world. Everyone will give an account for their life before the throne of heaven when it comes their time. God's purging fire will burn away all that is not of Him and what is left is the balance of the account for each life given. Jesus said that if we receive Him into our heart and acknowledge Him before this world and heaven, declaring Him our Lord and Savior He would acknowledge us before His Father. But if we deny Him and His gift of salvation He will deny us before the Father. You and I need to realize that His story of salvation is about us and our return to the Father through Him. It is all about everybody being part of the rest of the story. His story of love for all of us. As we are told us in the book of Hebrews, "Therefore as the Holy Spirit says, "Today, if you will hear His voice, Do not harden your hearts as in the rebellion, In the day of trial in the wilderness, Where your fathers tested Me, tried Me, And saw My works forty years. Therefore I was angry with that generation, And said, "They always go astray in their heart, And they have not known My ways." So I swore in My wrath, "They shall not enter My rest.". (Hebrews 3: 7-11). Hear His voice. Surrender to His Son Jesus the Christ and live. Lift up your head, look into His eyes of love and never turn away. Run into His loving arms and stay. Jesus the Christ calls you now. You will know the delight of His presence for always and share the company of His people both here in this life and into eternity.

Epilogue

This is the story of my walk of faith. It is far from being over. So much is yet to be learned. It has been a pleasure sharing it with you. Thank you. You are now part of the rest of the story.

I see my Father in heaven a little clearer each day as I walk with Him, and the closer I get to my last breath, the greater is the awe I have for His wonders.

Our walk in this life is as hard as we want to make it. Certainly, there are injustices we may endure, for sadly, we treat each other rather poorly. But still, we decide how we shall respond to all that is wrong and all the wrong that has come against us.

We are forgiven as we forgive others. And we do this not by our own strength of will but by the will of the Holy Spirit of Jesus. We cannot capture the wind in our hands, but we can hold the breath of God in our hearts and minds with welcome for Him to come in.

Life is very hard because of sin, but the chains of sin are broken by the power of His love and the cross.

You will learn who has always loved us by taking time to let love be in you in Him.

When you are afraid, remember that He has already been there.

When you are broken, He has already been there.

And when you are lost, He will safely lead you home.

My prayer for you: to know the fullness of His love here and now and forever.

This is God's promise to all creation for all time.

"Oh sing to the Lord a new song! For he has done marvelous things; His right hand and His holy arm have gained victory. The Lord has made know his salvation; His righteousness he has revealed in the sight of the nations. He has remembered His mercy and His faithfulness to the house of Israel; all the ends of the earth have seen the salvation of our God. Shout joyfully to the Lord, all the earth; Break forth in song, rejoice and sing praises. Sing to the Lord with the harp, with the harp and the sound of a psalm,

With trumpets and the sound of a horn; Shout joyfully before the Lord, the King. Let the sea roar and all its fullness, the world and those who dwell in it; Let the rivers clap their hands; let the hills be joyful together before the Lord, For he comes to judge the earth. With righteousness He shall judge the world, and the people with equity.". (Psalm 98: 1 -9 NKJV)

Lightning Source UK Ltd.
Milton Keynes UK
UKHW021019210820
368606UK00012B/911